DEDICATION

To the One who designed me intentionally and for His glory—
This book is for You, Lord, the Author of my story.

To every woman who has ever felt unseen, unworthy, or misunderstood—
May you discover the beauty of your unique design and walk boldly in your God-given purpose.

And to my family and friends who have loved, encouraged, and prayed for me throughout this journey—
Your support has been a reflection of His love.

INTENTIONALLY DESIGNED

ENDORSEMENTS

"I had the privilege of being Hannah's youth pastor, and got a front row seat to watch her grow into a passionate woman of God. *Intentionally Designed* is a heartfelt challenge to women to live boldly for Him and embrace their God-given purpose. This inspiring book reflects Hannah's deep faith and will empower readers to align their lives with God's plan. I couldn't be prouder of her."

-Jon Mahlstedt, pastor of Next Gen at Northbrook Church

"*Intentionally Designed* is not just a book—it's a roadmap for living with intentionality and faith. Hannah's practical steps and relatable stories make it accessible and impactful for women in every season of life. Don't just read this book—apply its truths and watch God work in your life!"

-Dr. Brian Dixon, founder of hope*writers

"*Intentionally Designed* is a beautiful expression of how God has created His children so purposefully. It is relatable, truthful, practical, and it displays how God will use your life for His glory. It has been a blessing to watch God use Hannah to further the Kingdom."

-Alison Hardy, Alison Hardy Photography

"Hannah and her book have encouraged me to step out in faith with the gifts God has given, reminding us that these gifts thrive the best in community! *Intentionally Designed* is going to show you that in Jesus, you will discover all the identity, purpose, and love you will ever need, and that YOU are intentionally designed by the King of all Kings! Get ready to find out how His power is always made perfect in our weaknesses. To Him be the glory!

-Lexi Hermes, author of *You Can, Through Christ*

INTENTIONALLY DESIGNED

Copyright ® 2026 by Hannah Castiaux
Published by UNITED HOUSE Publishing
All rights reserved. No portion of this book may be reproduced or shared in any form - electronic, printed, photocopied, recorded, or by any information storage or retrieval system, without prior written permission from the publisher. The use of short quotations is permitted.

Scripture quotations are from the ESV® Bible (The Holy Bible, English Standard Version®), © 2001 by Crossway, a publishing ministry of Good News Publishers. ESV Text Edition: 2025. The ESV text may not be quoted in any publication made available to the public by a Creative Commons license. The ESV may not be translated in whole or in part into any other language. Used by permission. All rights reserved.

ISBN - 978-1-952840-87-6
UNITED HOUSE Publishing Clarkston, Michigan
info@unitedhousepublishing.com www.unitedhousepublishing.com

Author Photograph: Alison Hardy Photography
Interior Design: Talitha McGuinness;
talitha@unitedhousepublishing.com
Printed in the United States of America 2025 - First Edition

SPECIAL SALES:
Most UNITED HOUSE books are available at special quantity discounts when purchased in bulk by corporations, organizations, and special interest groups. For more information, please email orders@unitedhousepublishing.com.

Ditching the lies and labels and living free in Christ.

INTENTIONALLY
designed

HANNAH CASTIAUX

INTENTIONALLY DESIGNED

CONTENTS

A Note To The Reader 9

PART ONE: Ditching the Lies + Labels 11

Chapter 1: From the Beginning 13

Chapter 2: Who Told You That? 31

PART TWO: Designed For This 45

Chapter 3: Designed For Relationship 47

Chapter 4: Designed To Cultivate 61

Chapter 5: Designed With Needs 73

Chapter 6: Designed With Purpose 89

Chapter 7: Designed With Gifts 97

Chapter 8: Designed To Co-Create 107

Chapter 9: Designed To Rest 117

Chapter 10: Designed To Worship 127

PART THREE: Living Boldly In Freedom 137

Chapter 11: Designed For Such A Time As This 139

Chapter 12: Designed For The Kingdom of God 147

Resources 154

INTENTIONALLY DESIGNED

A NOTE TO THE READER

For years, I wrestled with feeling I wasn't enough. I lived under the pressure to meet the expectations of the world, striving for perfection in all the wrong places. But as I began to lean into God's Word, I discovered a liberating truth: my identity, my purpose, and even my weaknesses were all part of His intentional design.

This book is a journey through the ways God has uniquely crafted us for a purpose far greater than we could imagine. Each chapter unpacks the layers of your God-given identity—your needs, gifts, ability to rest, calling to co-create, and more.

You'll also see how our design reflects the very nature of God. You weren't made to blend in, measure up, or live for the approval of others. You were made for such a time as this, for the Kingdom of God, and for His glory.

Throughout this book, we'll look at biblical truths, personal stories, and practical insights to help you embrace the way God has intentionally designed you.

If you've ever wondered if your story matters, if you have a purpose, or if God sees you, know this: He does. You were designed with love, purpose, and precision by the One who doesn't make mistakes.

Let this book be your invitation to step into your identity, live boldly for His Kingdom, and find rest in knowing you are exactly who God intended you to be.

You are intentionally designed.

INTENTIONALLY DESIGNED

PART ONE: DITCHING THE LIES + LABELS

INTENTIONALLY DESIGNED

Chapter 1: From the Beginning

I used to love beginnings—until I lived through a few. There's something magnetic about the start of a new season, a new chapter, or a fresh page that feels full of possibility. But, if I'm honest, beginnings also used to terrify me. Starting something new meant stepping into the unknown, but I liked certainty. I liked knowing where I was going, what the outcome would be, and how everything would unfold. I liked control, clarity, and clear plans with tidy endings wrapped up in a bow. But life doesn't work like a roadmap, and neither does faith. I remember a season when I felt completely lost, questioning where I fit and what God was doing in my life. I kept trying to piece together my own version of a plan, hoping that if I just worked hard enough or figured things out fast enough, I wouldn't feel so unsteady. The more I tried to control the outcome, the more exhausted I became. It was like trying to put together a puzzle without the picture on the box—frustrating, overwhelming, and at times, defeating. Then, in the middle of my striving, I sensed God whispering:

"Go back to the beginning."

At first, I didn't understand. But as I sat with those words, I realized something—before I could move forward, I had to go back. Back to the foundation. Back to where everything started.

Maybe you've felt this too. Maybe you've been in a season where you're trying to figure out your place, purpose, or next step. Maybe you're caught in the tension of wanting to move forward but feeling like you don't have

INTENTIONALLY DESIGNED

all the answers. Maybe you've felt the sting of shame when you realized you couldn't meet the expectations placed on you by your family, friends, yourself, or the culture we live in. Perhaps there have been times when you looked in the mirror, and the reflection didn't seem "enough"—not thin enough, pretty enough, or strong enough. You might have felt the weight of shame after making mistakes, as if your worth was tied to the illusion of perfection.

Some days, the voices of others—criticism from coworkers, friends, or even loved ones—echo in your mind, leaving you feeling small and unseen. Or perhaps shame crept in when your plans fell apart, leaving you questioning your ability, your value, or even your calling. There could have been moments when you felt judged for not fitting into the role you were expected to play—whether as a wife, mother, student, daughter, co-worker, athlete, or friend. **But where did this pressure to meet expectations begin?** For many of us, it wasn't one loud moment but a slow unraveling—subtle words, fleeting glances, or unspoken comparisons that planted seeds of doubt. Sometimes, all it takes is a single sentence, spoken at just the right moment, to shift how we see ourselves forever.

THE BIRTH OF A PEOPLE PLEASER

I remember the first day of my life when I didn't feel beautiful. I was in the fourth grade and was so excited to have my friends over to celebrate my tenth birthday. It was the most amazing sunny day in the middle of May in Wisconsin. Everywhere you looked was bright green, and the flowers were really starting to show off in bloom. I had picked out a lime green halter tank top, which I was so excited to wear for my birthday. I remember the excitement running through my veins as I waited to show off my new outfit at school and my birthday party. Life felt simple—until it didn't. That morning, a girl on the playground told me I was chubby. Compared to her, I

FROM THE BEGINNING

was much taller, which often made me wider than other girls, but I had never considered myself to be anything other than beautiful. I never considered myself chubby. I had never thought I needed to change anything about myself to be accepted by others. Until that moment, I was a carefree kid, never worrying about what others thought about me. This moment is when the "people pleaser" in me was born. I often wondered if I could regain my freedom of thought, but no matter what I did, I couldn't shake the constant concern about what others thought or felt about me. I had no idea I was entering the beginning of years of bondage, and the beginning of stories spiraling through my mind.

How quickly I went from wild and free to over-analyzing everything people said and did. I didn't realize the suffocating trap I had fallen into: people pleasing. I took pride in people liking me. What I didn't realize was that living for people's approval and opinions of me left me physically exhausted and mentally drained. I wondered if I could ever go back to feeling free in my mind, but no matter how hard I tried, I couldn't stop. I remember going to my birthday party and later looking at the pictures my family took on their digital camera; I didn't say a word about it to anyone, but I suddenly hated the pictures. I thought nobody would think I looked beautiful, and I must actually be chubby. I started critiquing the image of myself in my mind, but hid behind a smile. I started stuffing my feelings deep into the back of my mind and put on a mask, because I didn't want to bring anyone down and be a burden. I felt struck down by shame and believed that if I shared how I felt, I would be rejected, dismissed, and judged for my feelings. I felt paralyzed. I wish I could go back and hug my blonde, innocent self with glasses too big for my face and tell her, "It's not your fault."

But shame doesn't just show up in a single moment—it grows, weaving itself into our thoughts, choices, and the way we see ourselves. I didn't realize

INTENTIONALLY DESIGNED

then that this was only the beginning of a battle I would face for years, a battle between striving for approval and longing for freedom.

SHAME DOESN'T HAVE THE FINAL SAY

The enemy wants you to fall into the vicious cycle of believing there is shame in your story so you will give up on your calling and maybe even give up on God. The enemy wants you to experience deep shame because it's a part of his plan to steal, kill, and destroy your thoughts, your experiences, and truly your life. He wants you to feel stuck. He wants to distort the memories of what *actually* happened, twisting the truth just enough to make you question your worth, your role, or God's presence in the midst of it. He'll replay moments over and over in your mind, adding lies like, "It was all your fault," or "You should've known better," until the story you tell yourself is no longer rooted in truth but in shame, regret, and false guilt. He wants the story in your head to be tainted as to what *actually did* happen. Shame occurs when you feel you have done something wrong, triggering feelings of embarrassment, humiliation, and/or worthlessness that affect your identity and sense of value. Here's where the enemy gets crafty and what you need to know. There is a difference between recognizing a mistake and letting that decision define your identity and/or self-worth. We will make mistakes, but thank the Lord, our mistakes don't define us. God does.

If we're honest, some of us have believed the lie that it was safer to hide in our shame. We lived in our past regrets, believing that was all our story had to offer. Maybe you say, "It is what it is," or perhaps you've never been told it doesn't have to be this way anymore. From one soul-sister to another, I want you to know this: **Shame may have been a chapter of your story, but it doesn't have to be the whole book.**

FROM THE BEGINNING

The good news is that shame is not your identity—you were made for freedom. If you've experienced shame, then you may have also felt shame about the fact that you still feel shame or like you have to fight it constantly. You're not alone. The inner battle isn't new—shame has been a part of the human story since the very beginning. It all started in the Garden of Eden.

You've probably heard her name before, Eve. You know her, right? She often gets a bad rap, and most would blame her for the broken world we live in. But what if the story isn't just about shame or failure? What if, even in the fallout, God was already working a plan to restore our identity and call us back as His beloved?

The world constantly pushes us to chase the next thing—to build, hustle, and achieve—but in all that striving, it's easy to forget where we came from. When life feels overwhelming, when purpose feels unclear, when we start questioning our worth, we have to ask ourselves:

Have I forgotten the beginning?

From the very first pages of Scripture, we see that God is a God of beginnings. Genesis 1:1 says, "In the beginning, God created..." Before anything else, there was God, and out of His love, He created the world—and us. But here's what's incredible: Before God ever gave Adam and Eve a task, before He gave them instructions, before they did anything, He called them **His creation. His beloved.** Their identity wasn't based on what they did. It was based on *who they belonged to.*

"*God saw all that he had made, and it was **very** good.*"
Genesis 1:31

Before the fall, before the striving, before the shame, God looked at them—fully known and fully loved—and called them very good.

INTENTIONALLY DESIGNED

We see the enemy's first attack wasn't just on their actions—it was on their identity. In Genesis 3, when the serpent approached Eve, he didn't just question what God said. He planted doubt in her mind about *who she was*. About whether God's way was really good. About whether she was lacking something. That same attack continues today. The enemy doesn't always come at us with obvious lies; he comes with questions that make us doubt what God has already spoken.

"Did God really say...?"
"Are you sure you're enough?"
"Wouldn't life be better if you were in control?"

Just like that, we start forgetting the beginning. We forget that we were created in love, not in lack. We forget that our identity was given, not earned.

But the good news? Jesus came to restore what was lost in the garden. John 1:1 echoes Genesis: "In the beginning was the Word, and the Word was with God, and the Word was God."

Jesus **is** the beginning. He's the foundation. When we lose our way, He doesn't tell us to strive harder—He invites us to return to Him. As we lean into Him, He leads us back to our original design. Back to the Garden. Back to the place where our purpose was first planted.

THE GARDEN

"Let us make man in our image, after our likeness. And let them have dominion over the fish of the sea and over the birds of the heavens and over the livestock and over all the earth and over every creeping thing that creeps on the earth. So God created man in his own image, in the image of God he created him; male and female he created them. And God blessed them. And

FROM THE BEGINNING

God said to them, 'Be fruitful and multiply and fill the earth and subdue it, and have dominion over the fish of the sea and over the birds of the heavens and over every living thing that moves on the earth.' And God said 'Behold, I have given you every plant yielding seed that is on the face of all the earth, and every tree with seed in its fruit. You shall have them for food. And to every beast of the earth and to every bird of the heavens and to everything that creeps on the earth, everything that has the breath of life, I have given every green plant for food.' And it was so. And God saw that everything that he had made, and behold, it was very good. And there was evening and there was morning, the sixth day."
Genesis 1:26-28

After God created the earth and everything in it, He created mankind and called them **very good.** God created both male and female in the likeness of God, Jesus, and Holy Spirit. God blessed them and told them to be fruitful and multiply, fill the earth, and subdue it. He gave them dominion over the birds and animals on land and in the sea, and God told them about all the seeds and plants so they could eat.

"The Lord God took the man and put him in the garden of Eden to work it and keep it. And the Lord God commanded the man, saying, "You may surely eat of every tree of the garden, but of the tree of the knowledge of good and evil you shall not eat, for in the day that you eat of it you shall surely die. Then the Lord God said, "It is not good that the man should be alone; I will make him a helper fit for him". Genesis 2:15-16

Here, we see that God wants man to work and keep the garden. Right in the beginning, even in a place of perfect peace with the Lord, there was work to do. We also see that God gives the commandment not to eat of the tree of the knowledge of good and evil, and it is not good for man to be alone.

INTENTIONALLY DESIGNED

> *"So the Lord God caused a deep sleep to fall upon the man, and while he slept took one of his ribs and closed up its place with flesh, And the rib that the Lord God had taken from the man he made into a woman and brought her to the man. Then the man said, "This at last is bone of my bones and flesh of my flesh; she shall be called Woman because she was taken out of Man." Therefore a man shall leave his father and his mother and hold fast to his wife, and they shall become one flesh. And the man and his wife were both naked and were not ashamed."*
> Genesis 2:21-25

God put man in the garden to work in it because it wasn't finished. It was something that continuously needed to be tended. If we don't take care of a garden, we know what happens, right? Weeds sprout up. Plants die. The fruit diminishes. I am not a natural green thumb gal, but I'm learning, over time, that pulling up weeds gives the actual plant more opportunity to flourish. If you don't pull weeds out by the root, you spend even more time weeding, and sometimes they grow back worse. Taking care of a garden can feel like a ton of work, but God didn't create us to do it alone. God saw that it wasn't good for the man to be alone and created a helper. God knew community was necessary.

> *"I will make a helper fit for him."*
> Genesis 2:18b

We are created to help one another tend the gardens God has prepared in advance, knowing it is better to do it together than by ourselves, and there is no shame in that. When God said, "It is not good for man to be alone" (Genesis 2:18), He declared His intention to create a *helper*—a term that is often misunderstood. The Hebrew word for "helper" here is *EZER*, and it carries a far deeper meaning than simply an assistant or subordinate.

FROM THE BEGINNING

In fact, *EZER* is used throughout Scripture to describe God Himself as a strong and capable helper who rescues and supports His people.

"The Lord is my strength and my shield; my heart trusts in Him, and He helps (EZER) me."
Psalm 28:7

"We wait in hope for the Lord; He is our help (EZER) and our shield."
Psalm 33:20

The word *EZER* in Genesis 2:18 should not be viewed as a term of inferiority, but of strength and partnership. Women were created with this divine purpose: to stand alongside men as equal partners in God's mission by offering unique gifts, wisdom, and strength to the relationship.

This concept of *EZER* reminds us that God designed women to embody His qualities of care, strength, and presence. Women are called to help not from a place of weakness but from the powerful position of being image-bearers of God. Just as God helps His people by sustaining, guiding, and empowering them, women are called to bring those qualities into their relationships and communities. Being a helper is not a role of less significance; it is a role modeled after God Himself—a call to live out His heart of compassion and strength in the world.

This calling on each of us as an *EZER*—modeled after God's own nature—also reveals a profound truth about the way we are meant to live and work. God didn't just create us for relationships but for partnering together to cultivate the world around us.

The gardens of our lives are the areas of responsibility, relationships, and purpose God has entrusted to you. He literally created us in His image to

INTENTIONALLY DESIGNED

do this work, but not alone. Why? Because God knows that things go better together. When we isolate ourselves, we're more vulnerable to deception. Just like Eve in the garden, we can be lured into things that look good on the surface but ultimately lead us away from God's truth and into sin.

This is why God's design for partnership and community is so vital. When we try to do life on our own, we become vulnerable to the enemy's schemes. Just as Eve was deceived in the garden, the enemy's strategy remains the same today: he isolates us, sows seeds of doubt, and uses shame to keep us from walking in the fullness of God's purpose.

Eve was created to be *EZER*—a powerful, dynamic partner, designed to help rule the earth alongside Adam. She was made for purpose and strength, walking in the authority God gave her. But when she ate the fruit, shame came crashing in, and she let it define her. Instead of standing tall in her true identity, she let that shame weigh her down, believing that one mistake could change everything about who she was. She hid from God, wrapped up in the lie that her worth was now tied to her failure. Instead of owning her calling as *Ezer*—a force of strength and partnership with God—Eve bought into the narrative that she was unworthy, broken, and disqualified. The enemy sold her a lie, and she took it. She lost sight of the truth: her identity was never meant to be defined by her failure, but by the bold, unshakable purpose God designed for her from the start.

In the same way, God didn't design you to live bogged down by shame. He designed you for good, to flourish, and to play a vital role in His story. From the beginning, you were created to hear His voice and walk confidently in His direction, rooting your identity in Who you belong to.

FROM THE BEGINNING

Yet so many of us feel stuck. The enemy whispers lies that make us question whether we're truly hearing God speak or if we're even worthy of His guidance. Have you ever felt ashamed for wondering if that quiet nudge in your spirit was from God? Have you ever doubted whether you were heading in the right direction? Me too. Sadly, this is where I find most women today: caught in a never-ending cycle of doubt and shame, unsure of how to break free.

I think Eve felt the same way. When shame creeps into our hearts, it doesn't just cloud our view of God—it distorts the way we see ourselves and the relationships around us. This is why the enemy uses shame so effectively, but the truth is, shame has been a tool of the enemy since the very beginning.

> "Now the serpent was more crafty than any other beast of the field that the Lord God had made. He said to the woman, "Did God actually say, You shall not eat of any tree in the garden?" And the woman said to the serpent, "We may eat of the fruit of the trees in the garden, but God said, "You shall not eat of the fruit of the tree that is in the midst of the garden, neither shall you touch it, lest you die"' But the serpent said to the woman, "You will not surely die. For God knows that when you eat of it, your eyes will be opened and you will be like God, knowing good and evil." So when the woman saw that the tree was good for food, and that it was a delight to the eyes and that the tree was to be desired to make one wise, she took of its fruit and ate and she also gave some to her husband who was with her and he ate. Then the eyes of both were opened, and they knew that they were naked. And they sewed fig leaves together and made themselves loincloths.
> Genesis 3:1-7

In the Garden, Eve encountered the serpent's lies, manipulation, and deception, and wrestled with the

INTENTIONALLY DESIGNED

question, "Did God really say...?" We see how quickly the enemy sowed doubt and confusion, twisting God's words and intentions to deceive her.

So many times, I have doubted what God says to me because my mind keeps asking, "Did God really say that?" Maybe you've experienced this too, so here's one thing I want to encourage you to do: write it down immediately when you feel like God is speaking to you. That way, you can go back not only to remember but also to clarify, be obedient, and know if the enemy is trying to deceive you.

Here are a few things to remember:

We see how easily the enemy twisted God's words, taking something He had said to Adam and distorting it enough to create confusion and doubt. Whether it was a misunderstanding between Adam and Eve, or Eve's own interpretation, the point is this: how we hear God and how we repeat what He says matters. Miscommunication creates space for doubt. Clarity comes from knowing God's voice and trusting it above all else.

We weren't created to carry the weight of knowing everything. The enemy tempted Eve with knowledge, but it was intimacy with God that sustained her. Holiness doesn't come from having all the correct answers—it comes from knowing the right Person. Jesus.

This is where the story of shame began. Adam and Eve's eyes were opened, and suddenly, they felt exposed. In their panic, they reached for what was nearby—a fig leaf. I wonder if they grabbed it not just because it was available but because it was something God had made. Perhaps they believed that covering themselves with something "good" would conceal what had gone wrong. Isn't that what we do, too? We try to cover our shame with goodness—acts of service, achievements, relationships,

FROM THE BEGINNING

ministry—thinking it will make our sin invisible. But God doesn't ask us to hide. He invites us to repent and be restored.

> *"And they heard the sound of the Lord God walking in the garden in the cool of the day, and the man and his wife hid themselves from the presence of the Lord God among the trees of the garden. But the Lord God called to the man and said to him, "Where are you?" And he said, "I heard the sound of you in the garden, and I was afraid, because I was naked, and I hid myself." He said, "Who told you that you were naked? Have you eaten of the tree of which I commanded you not to eat?" The man said, "The woman whom you gave to be with me, she gave me fruit of the tree, and I ate." Then the Lord God said to the woman, "What is this that you have done?" The woman said, "The serpent deceived me, and I ate."*
> Genesis 3:18-13

So many of us are hiding in our shame from God, the one who already knows. Shame tells the lies, but conviction brings truth. I love how God is so gentle and knows where they are, but still asks them, "Where are you?"

When Adam answered, his words revealed something that never existed between him and God before: **fear**.

"I heard You in the garden, and I was afraid because I was naked, so I hid."

Have you ever felt exposed or found out? I cannot tell you how many times, as a kid, when I knew I did something wrong (believe it or not, I was a bit of a rebellious child), I'd hear my parents, and my neck would get this crazy tingly feeling. I would be low-key freaking out because I thought I was going to get into so much trouble.

INTENTIONALLY DESIGNED

What I love about Adam's response is that, **even in his fear, he was still honest.** He admitted what he felt: "God, for the first time ever, I was afraid of You. And I'm naked, so I hid." But, he stopped short of admitting the full truth. He didn't say, *I ate from the tree You told me not to.*" Yet, God, in His kindness, doesn't condemn. He simply asks, "Who told you that?"

Instead of taking responsibility, Adam shifts the blame: "The woman You gave to be with me—she gave me the fruit, and I ate." In one sentence, he not only blames Eve but subtly blames God, as if to say, "I didn't ask for her; You gave her to me, so really, isn't this Your fault?" How often does the enemy try to get us to do the same? To point our fingers at God when things go wrong?

Eve, on the other hand, admits she was deceived. But in that moment, both of them lost sight of who they were created to be. They went from walking in perfect communion with God to standing in the tension between shame and blame. Isn't that where we so often find ourselves?

Here's a question only you can answer:
Have you forgotten the beginning? Have you been caught in the cycle of trying to prove yourself, trying to figure everything out, trying to earn something that was already given? If you've been feeling lost, exhausted, or unsure of your purpose, maybe it's time to stop striving and go back: back to who God says you are, back to the truth that you were created from love, not for performance.

Because, from the very beginning, your worth was never about what you do—it was about *who you belong to*.

God, your *good* Father, intentionally designed every detail about you. You were made in His image, and He loves you. Chances are, you know what it's like to feel overwhelmed by all the labels or statuses and even lies

FROM THE BEGINNING

the world likes to throw at you. Maybe you've tried a few on because they sounded nice, but you later realized the lies you thought were the truth were actually shackles on your feet. **God's plan for you is freedom.** It always has been. His plan for you is Him. He is the abundance and the freedom and the hope and the joy.

Imagine if we actually lived like this. Imagine a generation of women who weren't striving for worth but walking in the identity given to them from the beginning. Women who didn't have to chase purpose because they knew they were already walking in it. What if, instead of feeling pressured to create our own plans, we trusted the One who has already written our story? Because here's the truth: The One who began a good work in you will be faithful to complete it (Philippians 1:6). He's the God of the beginning, the middle, and the end. No matter where you find yourself today, He's calling you back.

Back to rest.
Back to trust.
Back to Him.

This is where God gets the glory in your story.
Heavenly Father,

Thank you for being the Author of life and the One who has known us from the very beginning. In every moment of our story, You have been present, shaping us with intention, purpose, and love. As we reflect on the truth that we were created with divine care, may we be reminded that nothing about our lives is an accident. You designed us with a purpose long before we even understood who we were.

Lord, help us embrace the truth of who You say we are. Let Your voice drown out the lies we've believed about our identity, our worth, and our future. Guide us to walk in the freedom that comes from knowing we are fearfully and

INTENTIONALLY DESIGNED

wonderfully made, chosen to live out the calling You've placed on our hearts.

Teach us to trust You in every step of our journey, knowing that You've written each chapter with love, grace, and a hope-filled ending. May our lives bring glory to You, the One who began a good work in us and promises to carry it to completion.

In Jesus' name we pray,
Amen.

THIS IS WHERE GOD GETS THE GLORY IN YOUR STORY.

INTENTIONALLY DESIGNED

Chapter 2:
Who Told You That?

I remember sitting on my bedroom floor with my Bible open in front of me, heart heavy. I had hit a wall—not a physical one, but a wall made of exhaustion, frustration, and deep insecurity. I had spent years trying to do the right things—trying to be a good Christian, a good friend, a good leader. No matter how hard I worked, no matter how much I poured into others, there was this nagging feeling that it still wasn't enough.

Somewhere along the way, I bought the lie that if I could just be *more*—more disciplined, more accomplished, more likable—then peace would finally find me. But instead, I was exhausted. I was carrying a weight I couldn't name, but it was pressing on every part of me.

That night, I finally cracked open my questions before God. *Why do I always feel behind? Why do I keep striving when You've called me to rest? Why do I feel like I have to earn what You already gave me?*

And in the middle of that silence, I felt a gentle whisper settle into my soul.

"Who told you that?"

At first, I didn't know how to answer. Who told me I wasn't enough? Who made me believe my worth was something I had to earn? I could trace it back to specific moments—words spoken over me, cultural expectations, and pressures I had absorbed without realizing it. Suddenly, I saw it. I had been living under a weight God never put on me.

INTENTIONALLY DESIGNED

Maybe you grew up in a home where love felt like something you had to earn. Maybe success was celebrated, but your struggles were silenced. Maybe someone has told you your value is tied to your usefulness. Or maybe the culture around you convinced you that worth is measured by your productivity, beauty, or your ability to "keep it all together."

And let's be honest—sometimes even the church adds to this pressure. We hear messages about being a Proverbs 31 woman, or about living out our purpose with passion and grit. Those things are beautiful when rooted in truth, but without grace, they become just another measuring stick. Another place to fall short. Another voice whispering, *you're not enough.*

So, we hustle. We push ourselves to be more and do more to prove we are worthy of love, success, and a calling. But deep down, we wonder: *When will it be enough? When will I be enough?*

That's when we have to stop and ask the question: *Who told us we weren't already enough?*

The world is telling us in a million different ways who we are supposed to be while here on Earth. I believe God wants His daughters to know who He created them to be.

WHERE DID THAT COME FROM?

I remember waiting in line in gym class in the 6th-grade to be picked to play volleyball, and the girl in front of me turned around and asked me if I ever thought about getting a nose job. Ouch. I questioned my identity, already having struggled with feeling chubby in elementary school. She told me that if she were me, she would get a nose job because my nose was too big for my face. I went home that evening and asked my mom if I could get contacts

WHO TOLD YOU THAT?

and wear makeup. I started analyzing every part of my face, picking it apart because one girl shared her unfiltered, unsolicited opinion. I remember jumping from one thing to the next. Was my forehead too big? Did my glasses make me look like a child? Now, if you can relate to this story, all I can say is that I see and hear you, and I'm sorry this was ever said to you. I carried the pain of those words spoken over me in sixth grade in my back pocket until a few years ago. I hid behind the mask of makeup and contacts, and started caring way too much about the opinions others had of me. Carrying these words became very heavy until I fully surrendered them to God. (DISCLAIMER: This is not a book that says contacts, makeup, or style are bad. I've been shamed to death about a few of these things in life already, so let's breathe easily, knowing that this book is about being free in our identity in Christ and walking confidently in that. I wear makeup, I wear contacts, and I enjoy pulling my style together.)

The world loves to put lies and labels on us and convince us they are real. Does anybody else have blonde hair, or did they for a time? I was a blonde for years, and people had all kinds of nicknames for me. People relied on the dumb blonde jokes to be funny, but after a while, it can be easy to wonder if the words spoken over us are actually valid. "Hey, no offense, but I'm gonna share a blonde joke." "Hey, don't take this personally, but you remind me of the blonde in this joke." After a while, I began to wonder if I was dumb, just because they were called dumb blonde jokes. Maybe I was dumb because I didn't get through high school with A's, unless it was choir or gym class. I truly believed this lie for the longest time. I can still remember sitting in a classroom as a little girl, the sting of a classmate's voice echoing in my ears: "You're so dumb." Maybe they laughed when they said it, but it wasn't funny to me. I laughed too, just to fit in, but something shifted that day. I began to doubt my intelligence, speed, and overall capabilities. That one word—*dumb*—became a thread that wove itself into how

INTENTIONALLY DESIGNED

I approached school, friendships, and even my faith. I second-guessed my ideas, shrank back in conversations, and told myself to stay small so no one could point out what I already feared was true.

For years, I let these labels shape how I saw myself, allowing the names and jokes to sink deeper into my identity. Have you heard of personality tests? I'm an Enneagram three, and on the Myers-Briggs Test, I'm an ENFJ. I enjoy using personality tests as a tool for self-discovery, but I always seek the Lord first, ensuring that my identity is rooted in Him rather than in a test result. If you know anything about the Enneagram, the twos are known for being the HELPER, and for years, I truly believed that number described me to a T. I was always praised for being "Hannah the Helper." Still, I sacrificed so many things to help people, including eating, sleeping, and taking care of myself. I didn't know how to set good boundaries for myself and learn how to say no. I recently discovered I'm definitely more of a 3, and it all made sense. When I was called "Redders' Go-Getters," I couldn't quit. I had to go after everything with passion and zeal because a go-getter doesn't give up when the going gets tough. I felt I had to put on a brave face for everybody, except myself.

But then, I started exploring other ways of understanding who I was—ways that pointed more to how I was designed rather than how others saw me. I began opening the Bible not just for information, but for transformation. I began to look at what God said about me. Instead of believing I was unwanted or overlooked, I began to believe Psalm 139—that I was fearfully and wonderfully made, knit together by God Himself with intentional care. Instead of carrying the shame of my past, I read 2 Corinthians 5:17 and held onto the truth that in Christ, I was a new creation—the old had gone, and the new had come. Instead of being bound by the pressure to be perfect, I leaned into Ephesians 2:10, which reminded me I was God's workmanship, created in Christ Jesus to

WHO TOLD YOU THAT?

do good works He prepared in advance for me. When I doubted my worth, I remembered Romans 8:16—that I am not just a face in the crowd, I am a daughter of God, adopted into His family and given an eternal inheritance. These truths didn't just inspire me—they redefined me.

In high school, I started meeting with a wonderful mentor, Debbie. She knew I was a yes-girl. She challenged me to attend a student leader meeting for our youth group without volunteering, allowing others to take the lead. I was proud of being known as the girl who would always show up because, in reality, I feared letting people down. I sat and didn't make eye contact that Wednesday night. It felt so hard and awkward. I think people were shocked I didn't raise my hand. My heart was racing, and I kept thinking to myself, *Would someone please step forward?* And guess what? People did step up and volunteer. In those moments, I realized my identity had been wrapped up in being a helper, but if I was always the one saying yes, I was actually taking away opportunities for others to grow. The truth was, if I didn't do everything, someone else *would*. I needed to lay down the need to be needed at the feet of Jesus.

Let me ask you something—who told you that? Who made you believe your value has to be earned, your voice has to be quiet, or your presence has to be proven?

And before you even think about picking up shame—hear me clearly: this is not your fault. It's not your fault that others spoke words that didn't reflect the heart of God. It's not your fault someone used your insecurities as a weapon. It's not your fault that people projected their pain onto you. And it's certainly not your fault that those who were broken ended up breaking pieces of you, too.

You didn't deserve it. You weren't too sensitive. You weren't asking for it. You were simply a daughter of God in a broken world—and the things done to you were never

INTENTIONALLY DESIGNED

His design.

Hurt people, hurt people. Healed people, heal people, and freed people help break the chains.

If we aren't careful, the lies spoken over us can start to sound an awful lot like the truth. It can be so easy to start believing lies, especially if we are not rooted in the Word, knowing and understanding God, our Father and Creator, who He is, and what He says about us. But I want you to know you are not alone. There are so many women who are fighting similar battles and lies as you.

The enemy tends to attack our identity to keep us from living out the intentional design God created us for. I want you to sit here for a minute and breathe and ask the Holy Spirit to reveal to you the lies and labels you believe are true about yourself.

I will share a list of common lies and labels with you, and I want you to circle the ones you are struggling with right now. To fight the lies, we first have to admit that we might be believing a lie in our lives. We must acknowledge that God speaks life and truth over us, and He is the healer. Secondly, we have to ask ourselves: Who told you that? Thirdly, we must ask God, "What is the truth?"

I want you to know that healing does not always look like TikTok transitions. They can take time and effort, and look messy, but the first step is addressing that we are actually believing a lie. Ask yourself if you want to be healed from the lies you are believing.

- I'm stuck
- I'm not enough
- I'm too much
- My burdens are too much for other people
- I'm ugly
- There is nothing good about me
- I'm invisible
- Nobody understands me

WHO TOLD YOU THAT?

- I'm too far gone
- People are better off without me
- I'm better off dead than alive
- Since she's doing something similar, I should give up
- My anxiety disqualifies me
- I'm not doing enough
- I'm dumb
- I haven't experienced God like her
- I have to be put together perfectly
- Being misunderstood ruined my chance
- I'm alone
- Redemption isn't for people like me
- I'm unlovable
- I'm unworthy
- I'm not worth the time and energy
- I'm not worth celebrating
- I'm a failure
- My sin only affects me
- I'm a mistake
- I need human approval
- I'm rejected
- I'm a mess
- My broken parts can't be healed
- Everybody else is doing better than I and is more qualified

If you don't want to circle in your book, grab a journal and write down the lies you are believing. Feel free to write down some more of your own or more that come to mind.

WHAT THE ENEMY WANTS YOU TO BELIEVE

These lies aren't random—they're strategic. The enemy has been using the same script since the Garden.

"Did God really say You must not eat from any tree in the garden?"
Genesis 3:1

His goal is for you to question what God says to you, to question God's plan, to stop trusting Him, and to think that what the world has to offer you is better. SPOILER ALERT. The enemy never has our best interests in mind.

"The enemy comes to steal, kill and destroy, but I have come to bring life and life abundantly."
John 10:10

INTENTIONALLY DESIGNED

The enemy uses words to bring us down, never to build us up. We might think it is to build us up, but it's actually to make us believe we are somebody we aren't and question the One who created us. The enemy wants our identity to be built on temporary things as fragile as sand, so we crumble and don't walk in the identity and calling God has placed on our lives.

But there is always **HOPE.** We will explore this further in the chapters to come, but for now, this is what we want to stand on. Jesus is the word, and the word is the truth, and the truth sets us free.

"Jesus said to him, 'I am the way, and the truth, and the life. No one comes to the Father except through me.'"
John 14:6

"So Jesus said to the Jews who had believed in him, 'If you abide in my word, you are truly my disciples, and you will know the truth, and the truth will set you free.'"
John 8:31-32

Jesus is the Word, and the Word is the truth, and the truth will set you free.

Jesus is what sets you free. No one else can set you free, and nothing else can save you. The world loves to falsely promise us that once we achieve or receive the next job, pay raise, outfit, bigger house, or following, it will finally

- Organic Food
- Western Medicine
- Holistic Medicine
- Organized Home
- Minimalist Home
- Non-toxic Products
- The Government
- Your Savings Account
- Your Job
- Social Media
- Control
- Success
- Job Promotion
- Your Next Pay Raise
- Approval of Others
- Dopamine Rush
- Clothing
- Vehicle

WHO TOLD YOU THAT?

make our lives better. You may have seen some of these pursuits or have thought they were going to be the end-all, be-all for you.

THINGS THAT CANNOT SAVE YOU:
This does not mean all of these things are bad. It doesn't mean God can't give us these good gifts and have them be part of His way for us. It means we have to seek Him first. It means we need to trust He is actually who He says He is.

WHO IS OUR HEAVENLY FATHER?
God is a relational God. Perfectly 3-in-1 and 1-in-3. He wants a relationship with us. This is where the rubber meets the road, and if you never pick up this book again, it's ok. I want you to open your Bible and invite the Holy Spirit to read the Word of God with you, ask questions, and get to know your Heavenly Father. The Bible shares with us God's character and nature. Our good and gracious Father is loving. 1 John 4:7-8 says, "Beloved, let us love one another, for love is from God, and whoever has been born of God and knows God. Anyone who does not love does not know God, because God is love." We read that God is love, and as we read earlier, God is also truth.

So, how does this relationship with God impact the words spoken to us by others? When people speak into our lives—whether they are close friends, family members, or even strangers—it's important to filter their words through the lens of God's truth and love. This is why we must ask ourselves the following questions when someone speaks to us:

- **Is what was said BINDING me?**
- **Is what's being said CONDEMNING me?**
- **Is what was said CONVICTING me?**

God's truth will never condemn or bind you. It will always bring conviction that leads to growth, freedom, and transformation. As we learn to recognize His voice, we begin to discern the difference between what aligns with His nature and what doesn't.

Bondage makes you a slave. It keeps you trapped in a cycle, pulling you further from who you're meant to be. Bondage restricts you, limiting your potential and ability to live in the fullness of God's design for you. Bondage exploits your weaknesses, keeping you focused on past mistakes instead of the freedom Jesus died to give you.

Condemnation, on the other hand, steals hope. It says you are too far gone, there's no chance for redemption, and the mess you're in is too big for God to fix. Condemnation wants you to stay stuck in shame, believing that you can never change or be free.

But conviction? Conviction is a beautiful invitation. It doesn't shame you—it leads you to Jesus. Conviction doesn't weigh you down; it points you toward the truth and reminds you that you are loved, forgiven, and called. Conviction shows you there is always hope because Jesus is the answer.

Earlier, I had you go through a list of lies and labels you might be believing about yourself. Maybe you even added a few more to that list as we walked through it. You may still be struggling to shake those thoughts off and believe you're truly free from them. But listen—God's not done yet. **What you believe today is not the final word on your life.** His truth has the power to rewrite every lie, break every chain, and turn every label you've worn into a story of redemption.

You may feel stuck, but He is moving you toward the truth. And when you start living in that truth, everything changes.

WHO TOLD YOU THAT?

LET'S TRADE THE LIES FOR TRUTH

"The voice said the second time, 'What God has made clean you must not say is unclean'."
Acts 10:15

The words of others do not get to define what God has made pure. The enemy's lies hold no power over what God has set apart for His glory. You are made in His image—nothing and no one can rewrite that truth. Your worth is not up for debate, and it doesn't shift with your circumstances. Who God says you are remains unshaken, no matter what changes around you.

Just because you feel a certain way doesn't make it a fact. You feel the way you do for many valid reasons, but just because you feel that way doesn't mean it's true. We can be quick to judge others' intentions, motives, actions, patterns, rhythms, and so much more. While we can feel like we've got people figured out, I want to challenge you to stop writing stories in your head about people who have hurt you. I am the queen of writing stories in my head about others, and all it has done is steal my joy.

So Jesus said to the Jews who had believed him, "If you abide in my word, you are truly my disciples, and you will know the truth, and the truth will set you free."
John 8:31-32

So here is what we are going to do to fight the lies. We will acknowledge first that there are lies. Secondly, we are going to replace the lies with the truth. That means getting into the Bible and reading the truth written about you and me. Thirdly, we are going to abide in Christ. His grace is sufficient for you, and His power is made perfect in our weaknesses.

THE POWER OF WORDS
Words have power. Words can either build up or

INTENTIONALLY DESIGNED

tear down. I believe God designed us to be able to speak and communicate because He is a relational God, and we are created in His image. God SPOKE, and the world was formed. He could have blinked, and He could have drawn it, but he chose to SPEAK.

Genesis 1:1-3 says, "*In the beginning, God created the heavens and the earth. The earth was without form and void, and darkness was over the face of the deep. And the spirit of God was hovering the face of the waters. And God said 'Let there be light, and there was light.*"

Time and time again, God speaks and creates things. But when God speaks, it is always good. Good for His glory and for the good of people.

When I was on staff at YWAM DENVER, my now husband, Steve, asked if I wanted to play basketball with him and a few of our friends. I said yes, excitedly, because, at the time, I had a huge crush on him. So, how could I say no? Long story short, I passed the ball to my friend and fell to the ground. I was embarrassed because I didn't even do anything cool. I literally just fell to the ground and soon realized my left knee was three times the size of my right knee. I had burst the bursa sack, and my kneecap shifted over. It hurt pretty badly. At the time, I was on the kitchen staff and would have to go to Sam's Club every week to pick up groceries. I felt utterly defeated and wondered how I could possibly do my job. Steve gave me a bracelet that said, "Embrace the Suck." He told me that even though I was injured, and it sucked, who I was in Christ didn't change at that moment. (Ok, do you see why I married this man?) Steve pointed me to the truth from the beginning. He reminded me that my worth didn't change when my ability to walk changed. He reminded me that my worth was rooted in God's word and what He says about me, not my injuries.

What God says of us is who we are. There's a reason

WHO TOLD YOU THAT?

He says so many things about our personhood in the Bible, and we can rest in the fact that God doesn't change.

- A Child of God
- Justified & Redeemed
- No Longer a Slave to Sin
- Accepted by Christ
- Adopted as His Own
- New Creation
- Chosen, Holy, and Blameless
- More Precious than Rubies
- Fearfully & Wonderfully Made
- Bold & Confident
- Righteous & Holy
- Citizen of Heaven

When God said, "Let there be light," in the beginning, I don't believe the light ever stopped being created. When sperm and an egg meet, a light goes off. There are thousands of stars continuing to be formed every single day. God said, "Let there be light," and it continues to be formed every second as He speaks love over us. The words He has already spoken over you don't change; they keep going on for eternity. Let's take some time to remember the words God has already spoken over us.

Who Does God Say You Are?

"How precious are your thoughts about me, O God. They cannot be numbered! I can't even count them; they outnumber the grains of sand! And when I wake up, you are still with me!"
Psalm 139:17-18

I know this is a lot of words, and you might still be saying, "Hannah, I don't feel this way. I don't think it's true. I am not the person He is talking about." But I want to gently remind you that you don't have to ACHIEVE your worth or identity. What if instead of walking towards achieving our worth and identity, we walked FROM our place of identity and worth in Christ? Your identity isn't something you achieve but something you receive. The enemy wants you to believe that achieving your identity is essential, so

INTENTIONALLY DESIGNED

you exhaust yourself trying to become this perfect version of yourself.

We don't need to strive to please God. He is already pleased with you. He already delights in you. He already loves you. Why? Because you are His child. So, are you going to believe the lies and the labels? Or are you going to believe the truth that will set you free?

You're not who the world says you are. You're not who your past says you are. You are who God says you are. Period. And starting today, you get to walk in that truth. HERE WE GO!

Father God,

Thank you for being the voice of truth in my life. In moments when I've believed lies about who I am, what I'm capable of, or how You see me, remind me of Your Word that speaks life, purpose, and identity over me. Help me to discern between Your voice and the lies of the enemy. Break the power of every false narrative I've accepted and replace it with Your truth. Lord, when I'm tempted to doubt my worth or question Your goodness, let Your Spirit guide me back to the assurance that I am fearfully and wonderfully made in Your image. Teach me to stand firm in what You say about me and reject any thought or label that doesn't align with Your truth.

In Jesus' name,
Amen.

PART TWO: DESIGNED FOR THIS

INTENTIONALLY DESIGNED

Chapter 3: Designed for Relationship

2020 was a hard year for all of us. The world shut down. Quarantine became the new normal, and we were told to isolate ourselves from the people we loved most. Everything felt uncertain. Everything got quieter. Lonelier. And while we turned to screens to stay connected, something deeper was missing. 2020 was exhausting, and praise God, we made it through.

For my family, 2020 was a whirlwind. Before the pandemic started, Steve and I had just found out we were pregnant with our first child. We were overjoyed. It was our first year of marriage, and we were living in California at the time. I was already struggling to meet people and wondering, *Where do Christian adults even make friends outside of church?* California felt so different from Wisconsin. Thankfully, I met a few sweet women through church and work, but I went from a tight-knit community to knowing almost no one. Add a pandemic to that, and I felt like I was unraveling.

My parents were planning to fly out to visit us, but the day before they were to leave, the state of California shut down, and their flights were canceled. I hadn't told my parents we were pregnant yet because I wanted to tell them in person when they got off the plane. I went to the nearest grocery store and bought as much food as I could find left on the shelves after everybody else went into a panic and bought everything, especially the toilet paper. If you know, you know. I called my parents via Facebook Messenger that night and bawled my eyes out as I felt this moment to share such happy news was

INTENTIONALLY DESIGNED

stolen from me. I told them the news, but it was nothing like the announcement I had envisioned.

As my pregnancy progressed, life became increasingly difficult. I was diagnosed with hyperemesis gravidarum and had to get IV fluids three times a week. I lost twenty pounds instead of gaining weight. I was too sick to work. Church was shut down. Our friends were far away. I felt completely alone.

Have you ever felt that kind of alone?

Later that summer, my parents rescheduled their trip, but days before they arrived, I was rushed into emergency surgery. We thought we were losing our daughter, but it turned out to be my appendix. The doctors said if we had waited any longer, we could've lost both her and me. My mom changed her flight and came out early to help. Steve and I started praying about whether we were supposed to stay in California or move closer to family.

Then our pastor's mom, Nancy, called. She said, "I felt God tell me you're supposed to be near your family right now in this season of your life." I burst into tears. It had been so long since someone else had heard from God on my behalf. The confirmation was clear—God was speaking. And He was using the community to do it.

WE WEREN'T MEANT TO DO LIFE ALONE

From the beginning, God made it clear: *It is not good for man to be alone.* (Genesis 2:18). We were designed in the image of a relational God—Father, Son, and Holy Spirit. God created the garden not just for function but for *fellowship*. He walked with Adam and Eve. He *dwelt* with them. He designed us to live in relationship with Him and each other.

God didn't just stop at the Garden. He sent Jesus to

DESIGNED FOR RELATIONSHIP

walk among us. He tore the veil so we could have direct access to Him. And He placed His Spirit inside us to remind us: *I am with you always.*

> *"Let us make man in our image, after our likeness."*
> Genesis 1:26

WE START TO LOOK LIKE WHO WE SPEND TIME WITH

Right off the bat, we know we are created in God's image, and part of His image is that God is relational. **We serve a God of connection**. He is speaking, and He is with us. He wants to connect with us.

You can know a lot *about* someone and still not actually *know* them. You might follow someone online, watch their stories, like their posts—but that doesn't mean you know their heart. Still, we do this with people... and sometimes even with God.

The enemy would love for us to settle for *facts* about God instead of a *relationship* with Him. He doesn't mind if we go to church or read a devotional now and then as long as we don't actually know God intimately. But Jesus didn't come to hand us a rulebook. He came to hand us *Himself*.

Knowing God is personal. It's daily. It's relational. Just like with any relationship, the more time you spend together, the more you start to reflect each other.

As a mom of three beautiful kids—Denver, Dallas, and Drake—I've learned this firsthand. I remember waiting to see what they'd look like. When I finally saw their faces, I thought, *Seriously? They look just like their dad!* (Haha, of course.)

Now that they're growing up, I've started noticing patterns: Our youngest looks a lot like me. Our oldest acts like me. And our middle one? He tries to be like me—

INTENTIONALLY DESIGNED

copying what I say, what I do, and how I move.

There's something powerful about being reflected. When we spend time with God, we begin to reflect Him. We talk like Him. We walk like Him. We love like Him. That's what holiness is—not perfection, but proximity. The more time you spend in God's presence, the more you'll start to resemble your Father.

BELONGING

Before God calls us to change, serve, or grow, He calls us to *belong*. God wants you to know that He knows you. He sees every detail of your life. He knit you together in your mother's womb. He knows the number of hairs on your head. He's caught every single one of your tears in a jar. Before you ever performed, produced, or proved anything, *you belonged.*

There's room for you in His Kingdom, yet so many of us are sitting ourselves out of the game—disqualifying ourselves before we've even stepped onto the field.

I often look at my kids, and I feel like God teaches me so much about Himself while I'm learning how to parent. Sometimes, we look at God only in an *"I have to do things perfectly"* kind of way because we are afraid we will get into trouble, and maybe that's how you felt growing up. I remember not wanting to get in trouble, even though I always got caught. My mom always knew things before I even tried to hide them. But honestly, I think of how I look at my kids, even though they mess up and make mistakes. To me, they're perfect because they're mine. They belong. They have a safe place to be themselves. I believe that's how God sees us, too. He's not waiting for you to clean yourself up or finally *"get it right."* He's your Father. His arms are wide open. He's your safe place. He's your home. However, for some of us, we learned to see God through the lens of fear—afraid we'd be in trouble if

DESIGNED FOR RELATIONSHIP

we got it wrong. Maybe you were raised to avoid mistakes at all costs. I get it—I was that kid too.

Here's what I've learned along the way. Belonging isn't about performance; it's about identity.

You belong because He says you do.
You are safe because He is good.
You are loved because He is love.

AFTER BELONGING COMES HEART CHANGE

Belonging is where it starts, but transformation is where God leads us next. When we truly begin to understand who we are in Christ, something shifts. Our hearts soften. Our vision clears. We begin to change—not because we're striving to be better, but because we're rooted in love. We can quickly discern what's counterfeit when we know what we believe. When we know God Himself, we recognize the false gospels and lies the enemy tries to slip in. This doesn't happen by simply learning facts *about* God; it happens by experiencing His character, love, and nature firsthand. It's when we encounter His heart that the Word begins to come alive in ways we never imagined.

It's one thing to hear *about* God. It's another thing to *know* Him.

We live in a world that worships independence.

"Be your own boss."
"Do you."
"Cut off anyone who doesn't serve your peace."

It sounds empowering on the surface, but underneath, it often leads to isolation. Culture tells us that self-sufficiency is strength, and relying on others is

INTENTIONALLY DESIGNED

weakness. You were created for relationship, not self-preservation. For community, not control. Godly community isn't just about having people around to hype you up—it's about having people who *call you higher,* people who will speak the truth to you when you forget who you are, people who will pray with you, challenge you, and remind you of the hope you have in Jesus. Because growth doesn't happen in isolation. Freedom doesn't happen in hiding, and healing rarely occurs alone.

In today's world, we've become a grace-centered generation—and that's amazing! Grace is at the core of the gospel, but there's a point where grace can become enablement. It's easy to fall into the trap of thinking grace means we can do whatever we want without consequences. However, sin is still destructive, and the enemy loves to convince us it's no big deal. The truth is, sin always leads to destruction, whether we see it right away or not.

I'll be honest—sometimes I think I've got it all under control. I'll think, "I've handled that sin, I'm good." But the truth is, none of us can handle sin on our own. It's easy to fall into pride and think we've got it covered, but the Bible is clear: "Pride comes before the fall." We all need accountability. **None of us is exempt.**

I don't like being called out. Who does? It's uncomfortable, and it can be painful. But the reality is, when we refuse to let others speak into our lives, we stay stuck. Accountability is what keeps us from staying in the same place of sin, and it's what helps us walk into the freedom Christ died for us to experience.

Being held accountable is counter-cultural. We live in a world that screams, "Do whatever you want." We've let culture shape our view on how we handle sin. We're told that our sin is *personal,* that confession is *optional,* and that as long as it's "just between me and God," we're

DESIGNED FOR RELATIONSHIP

fine. But here's the truth: hidden sin doesn't free you. It binds you.

Accountability is the light switch. We think that if nobody knows our sin, then we are safer and freer, but the reality is that the sin that is hidden binds us up. There are many reasons we might not share our sin—shame, fear of rejection, consequences of our actions, or fear of judgment. You are not accountable to everyone. You are accountable to God and whoever you permit to be that person in your life.

It's not about being punished—it's about being set free. It's not about shame—it's about sight. Because when you're walking in the dark, how do you see the danger in front of you? You turn on the light.

"Stay alert! Watch out for your great enemy, the devil. He prowls around like a roaring lion, looking for someone to devour."
1 Peter 5:8

The enemy isn't playing games. He doesn't care about your intentions. He's not passive. He's hunting. So we've got to stop fighting alone.

Accountability is how we fight back. It's how we expose the enemy's schemes. It's how we walk toward freedom. We weren't meant to carry our burdens alone. James 5:16 says,

"Confess your sins to each other and pray for each other so that you may be healed."

Not ashamed. Not canceled. **Healed.**

One time, I was arguing with Steve about something he didn't do—something I had expected him to do, and I thought I had asked him to do it. He said, "Hannah, sometimes when you ask me to do something, you are so vague about what you want. How am I supposed to know that's what you meant if you aren't specific?" If I didn't have Steve in my life to love me enough to tell me that, I could have interactions with others, thinking I'm being very specific, but in reality, I'm being really vague. If I didn't have people in my life correcting me in truth and love, how would I see my blind spots? Look, we have to get past the fact that it feels awkward. We need hearts that can't be easily offended. The enemy wants you to isolate yourself and never confess your sins to one another. He wants you to believe it is safer alone in the dark.

1. We need to be accountable to God. He is our savior. We need Him. Hebrews 4:13 says this: "Nothing in all creation is hidden from God, everything is naked and exposed before his eyes and he is the one to whom we are accountable."

2. We need to be accountable to one another. James 5:16 says this: "Confess your sins to each other and pray for each other so that you may be healed. The earnest prayer of a righteous person has great power and produces wonderful results."

If we have nobody to hold us accountable, then every decision we make is based on an emotion or a personal experience we only see through our individual worldview. Accountability shows us there is more than one side to every situation. It calls us out of darkness into the light. We were made to live in the light. It allows our eyes to be opened to the truth, which sets us free. Remember, **Jesus is the Word, and the Word is the truth, and the truth sets us FREE.**

Have you ever seen somebody cut a tomato? A dull blade makes it a lot harder to cut through a piece of fruit. Cutting with a dull knife is more dangerous than cutting with a sharp knife. You have a higher

DESIGNED FOR RELATIONSHIP

chance of hurting yourself. **That's what life looks like without accountability.** We think we're fine. But without sharpening, we're more likely to hurt ourselves and others.

"Iron sharpens iron, and one man sharpens another."
Proverbs 27:17

    I used to run a small interior design business and use social media for my marketing because, to be honest, it's free. I used to feel I must constantly produce content, and it took me a while to see how it was starting to control my life in a certain way. I was short with my husband. I always had to get the video or the photo. I'd get angry if something weren't done a certain way. I look back and see how silly I was acting. That summer, I decided to take a break from social media and found some close God-fearing friends who agreed to hold me accountable for three months. As the days went on, I saw so much more about my heart. My motives. The damage that was done. Where I placed my worth. My reputation. (Y'all, there were times, out of habit, that my finger would touch the app to open it up without me even thinking, but this book isn't just about social media, so we will save that for another day.)

    I was chatting with the friends I shared this with, and they said, "Why don't you just delete the apps then so you don't get tempted?" Accountability isn't just about confessing when you mess up; it's also about developing self-control, breaking chains, fighting a battle, and replacing lies with the truth. It takes action and patience to seek God intentionally and what He has to say to you. All of our sins and struggles start with a root. If you want to understand what He is saying, I recommend opening the good book we all know, the Bible. The Word is a gift.

    I needed to take action to keep myself accountable. Many of us like to declare the boundaries we are setting, but true freedom begins when we take action to make them a reality. I could've lied to my friends and told them

INTENTIONALLY DESIGNED

that I never hit the apps, or I could tell them the truth and have them help me do something about it. It's so simple, but we must be humble enough to admit it. It's okay to need help with accountability. Proverbs 19:20 says this: *"Get all the advice and instruction you can so that you will be wise the rest of your life."*

1. You were made to live in the light. Turn the light on so you can see the enemy's schemes in your life.

2. Stay alert. Practice self-control and discipline. Have people hold you accountable.

We are image bearers preparing His Bride to be holy and blameless. Accountability leads us to repentance and humility, which ultimately leads us to Jesus and freedom.

One of my favorite quotes is this: *"If you want to go fast, go alone. If you want to go far, go together."* - African Proverb

Together, we can go farther for the kingdom of God. Accountability has the opportunity to shape us more into the image of God. It's painful to be sharpened and forged in the fire. But it's not about how we feel, y'all. It is about making sure we are image bearers of Christ, walking humbly so that others can be saved and know Him. Jesus is coming back. We are one day closer today, and we need to prepare the bride of Christ, His church, but many of us are getting in the way. How far do you think the disciples would've gotten if they tried to spread the gospel alone— without community, accountability, or a team to run with? Here's something I want you to do: Find someone in your life whom you trust and who loves Jesus, to hold you accountable. And it could look something like this:

Hey Joe, I'm really struggling with _____. Would you be willing to meet with me and help hold me accountable?

DESIGNED FOR RELATIONSHIP

Here are my recommendations:

1. Have someone hold you accountable who is older and wiser, not somebody struggling with the same thing as you.

2. Have somebody of the same sex as you, so you aren't crossing boundaries.

I want you to message or call that person right after you put this book down. Don't wait. The book will be here when you're ready to come back to it. If you wait, you won't do it. Don't waste time and let the enemy come at you with more lies to keep you from the freedom that God paid for you on the cross.

Here's the thing. You were designed for relationships. You were designed for a relationship with God, and you were designed for relationships with people. If you think it is better to be alone because nobody understands you, that is a lie from the pit of hell. That lie is only going to leave you feeling more alone and isolated. Now, I'm not saying it's wrong if you've ever felt alone or if you don't feel understood. Many people I know are struggling with suffering and feel alone. But the truth is, you aren't alone. God is with you.

Even if you don't know anybody walking through the same season as you, you're not alone. I want to encourage you: **people don't have to understand your season to show up for you**. It's your choice whether you let them or not. I see so many people only want help from people who understand their season, versus someone who just wants to love them.

One of my friends is in a completely different time of life than I am. When I met her, she was single and running a photography business. I was a mom to two with a third on the way. She and I could easily relate because we both loved a crispy Dr. Pepper. We didn't have many of the same things going on in our lives, but our friendship proves that you don't have to be in the same season of life to show up intentionally. I started asking her if she'd like to come over for lunch or join me while I shopped for groceries. Over a year's time, we got to know each other so well because we invited each other to do life together. I pray you can just invite someone into the messy or mundane moments, and receive the love God has for you through imperfect people.

I've also had friends I've shown up for repeatedly, and they never returned effort, and our friendship slowly drifted apart. It was hard for me for a while, to be honest, but I understood that we were in different seasons of life; sometimes friendships are seasonal. This might be a good reminder to catch up with a friend you haven't seen or spoken to in a while. A message can go a long way since we don't always know what's happening in everyone's world.

I also have friends who are in a similar season of life as I am. One way we've stayed connected is through the Marco Polo app. It's kind of like video messaging—you record a message, and they can watch it whenever they have time. As a mom, it's hard always to be available for phone calls or long text threads, so this has made it easier to keep in touch. I love that I can hear their voices and see their faces—it helps things feel more personal, even when life is busy.

VULNERABILITY

What is the first thing you think of when you hear the word vulnerability? Does it make you cringe? Most people don't want to go first because they are scared to actually be fully known. Vulnerability happens best and safest in relationships. Vulnerability is the birthing room for growth, depth, and connection, but if it isn't protected,

DESIGNED FOR RELATIONSHIP

it can be used as a harmful tool. Many people have seen vulnerability gone wrong, which breaks my heart. But Jesus Himself came as a vulnerable baby. He needed someone to birth him, feed him, change his diaper, and hold him when he cried. He needed to be protected and cared for. **Let's be a safe place for others to belong. Then, we can hold each other accountable and continue to grow in depth through vulnerability.**

- Ideas for Connecting with People:
- Invite someone over for dinner
- Invite someone to go grocery shopping with you
- Invite someone to go to your kid's sporting events with you
- Invite someone to a church event with you
- Chat with people on the Marco Polo App
- Grab a coffee and pay for theirs
- Go on a walk or to the gym
- Invite someone over to help you with tasks like cleaning, doing the dishes, and laundry.

Loving Father,

Thank You for designing me for a relationship with You and with others. I am grateful that You created me to live in connection, not isolation. Help me to cultivate relationships that honor You and reflect Your love. Teach me to be patient, kind, and forgiving, just as You are with me. When relationships are difficult, give me the grace to persevere and to seek peace.

Most of all, Lord, draw me closer to You. Let my relationship with You be the foundation of all others. Fill me with Your love so I can love others well, knowing that I am never alone because You are always with me.

In Jesus' name,
Amen.

INTENTIONALLY DESIGNED

Chapter 4:
Designed to Cultivate

Imagine the most beautiful garden you've ever seen, bursting with vibrant colors and abundant life, tended with such detail and a gentle hand. Each plant is perfectly placed and nurtured in hopes of reaching its fullest potential. Just like a garden needs a gardener, your life, relationships, and calling need tending. You were *designed to cultivate*—to grow what's been planted in you and steward what God has entrusted to you. This chapter is your invitation to step into that calling.

One of the first things God did was create a garden, **but the Garden of Eden wasn't finished**. God created it and said that it was all very good. It was ready. It was prepared, but it needed somebody to cultivate it. Genesis 2:5 says this:

"When no bush of the field was yet in the land and no small plant of the field had yet sprung up-for the Lord had not caused it to rain on the land, and there was no man to work the ground, and a mist was going up from the land and was watering the whole face of the ground- then the Lord God formed the man of dust from the ground and breathed into his nostrils the breath of life and the man became a living creature. And the Lord God planted a garden in Eden, in the east, and there he put the man whom he had formed. And out of the ground the Lord God made to spring up every tree that is pleasant to the sight and good for food. The tree of life was in the midst of the garden and the tree of the knowledge of good and evil."

INTENTIONALLY DESIGNED

Think of your life like a garden. You may not have a green thumb, but you're still a gardener—because God has placed things in your life that are meant to grow. The question isn't *if* you're cultivating something. The question is: *what are you cultivating?*

The Bible mentions gardens over sixty times. This isn't a random theme—it's a visual God uses to teach us something deeper. Gardens require intention. So does your life.

CULTIVATION = STEWARDSHIP + DISCIPLESHIP

- Stewardship means taking care of what God has entrusted to you. You protect it, nurture it, and treat it like it matters—because it does.

- Discipleship is walking with others toward Jesus. It's coaching, encouraging, and challenging people to grow in faith—starting with your own.

Cultivation begins in your heart. You can't pour into others if you're running on empty. You can't lead someone where you haven't gone. That's why tending your own garden—the soil of your soul—matters so much. When your life is rooted in God, growth overflows into everything else: your relationships, your purpose, your impact.

God's goal isn't just for your life to look good—it's for it to bear fruit. And not just any fruit, but fruit that lasts.

"I am the true vine, and my Father is the vinedresser. Every branch in me that does not bear fruit he takes away, and every branch that does bear fruit he prunes, that it may bear more fruit. Already you are clean because of the word that I have spoken to you. Abide in me, and I in you. As the branch cannot bear fruit by

DESIGNED TO CULTIVATE

itself, unless it abides in the vine, neither can you, unless you abide in me. I am the vine; you are the branches. Whoever abides in me and I in him, he it is that bears much fruit, for apart from me you can do nothing. If anyone does not abide in me he is thrown away like a branch and withers; and the branches are gathered, thrown into the fire, and burned. If you abide in me, and my words abide in you, ask whatever you wish, and it will be done for you. By this my Father is glorified, that you bear much fruit and so prove to be my disciples."
John 15:1-8

That word **prune** can feel sharp. It sounds painful—and sometimes it is. But pruning isn't punishment. It's care. It's God removing what's holding you back so you can grow more deeply, fully, and freely.

Cultivation starts with *abiding*—staying connected to the Source. You can't produce fruit on your own. You weren't meant to. Fruit is the result of a relationship.

NOT EVERYONE HAS A GREEN THUMB (and that's ok)

Can I be honest with you? I used to hate gardening—mostly because it meant pulling weeds. Anybody else? Funnily enough, I ended up working a couple of landscaping jobs in my teens. Then a few years ago, I decided to grow watermelons because . . . well, they're the best fruit ever, and I figured I'd save a few bucks if I grew my own. Well, it turned out that my watermelon only grew to the size of a **golf ball.** I now stick to buying my melons and growing cucumbers instead.

Here's the point: **Not everyone is gifted at everything, and that's a good thing.**

When God created Adam to tend the garden, He didn't leave him to do it alone. He created Eve—a helper, a co-cultivator. Because we were never meant to build,

INTENTIONALLY DESIGNED

grow, or live in isolation. Each of us has different strengths. Different gifts. When we come together, we can cultivate more than we ever could alone.

At its core, stewardship is about love. It's not just about managing resources or responsibilities—it's about loving what God loves and treating it like it matters. And what does God love?

"For God so loved the world, that he gave his only Son, that whoever believes in him should not perish but have eternal life."
John 3:16

Since we love God, we learn to love what He loves. Since God loved the whole world so much that He sent His son to die for it, we learn to love the world because we love Jesus. Because He loves the world, we tend the physical gardens and His people.

Your garden might be your marriage. Your family. Your small group. Your church. Your classroom. Your workplace. Your online platform.

Whatever it is, God has entrusted it to you, and He's asking you to tend it in love.

Jesus used gardening language too—because He knew we'd need a picture of what real growth looks like. In Matthew 13, He tells the parable of the sower, describing how different types of soil affect the way seeds grow.

Here's a quick recap:

"A sower went out to sow. As he sowed, some seeds fell along the path, and the birds came and devoured them. Other seeds fell on rocky ground... but they had no depth, so they withered. Others fell among thorns, and the thorns choked them. But some fell on good soil and

DESIGNED TO CULTIVATE

produced grain—some a hundredfold, some sixty, some thirty."
Matthew 13:3-8

Jesus explained this parable later:

- The **path** is a hard heart—one where the seed doesn't even get a chance to sink in.
- The **rocky soil** represents people who receive the word with joy but fall away when things get hard.
- The **thorns** are distractions—the cares of life, the deceitfulness of riches.
- And the **good soil**? That's a heart ready to receive truth, hold onto it, and bear fruit.

Now think about this in your own life: Your heart is a garden. *What kind of soil is there right now?*

And not just in general—because your life is made up of different *"plots."* The soil in your **home** might be different from the soil in your **workplace**. Your **friendships** might be thriving while your **marriage** feels dry. Each area is worth examining.

God doesn't expect perfection, but He's inviting you to tend to the soil, clear out what's choking the truth, and prepare the ground for growth.

If your life is a garden, how do you care for it? How do you help the soil stay healthy, the seeds grow deep, and the fruit actually last?

Let's break it down—step by step.

1. Choose a Gardening Space

The first step? Start *somewhere*. Don't get overwhelmed thinking you need to change everything overnight. Ask God, *Where are You calling me to focus right now?*

INTENTIONALLY DESIGNED

Your garden could be your marriage. It could be your workplace. It could be your neighborhood, your kids, your small group, or even your own heart. Mission work isn't just about going overseas—it starts right where your feet are planted.

"Go therefore and make disciples of all nations, baptizing them in the name of the Father and of the Son and of the Holy Spirit, teaching them to observe all that I have commanded you. And behold, I am with you always, to the end of the age.".
Matthew 28:19-20

Here's a shift: don't just see it as a workplace. See the people. See the names, the faces, the souls. They aren't just co-workers—they're image-bearers who need the hope you carry.

Start with the people right in front of you. Your mission is people, and your life is the field. The Great Commission wasn't just for pastors or missionaries—it's for every single one of us. We go with God to make disciples wherever we are. Whether it's across the world or across the hall, your mission is people, and it starts right where your feet are planted.

2. Till the Soil

Before anything can grow, the ground has to be broken. Tilling stirs up the soil, makes space for air and water to move, and prepares it for new growth. In your life, that looks like being honest about what's working, what's not, and where your heart has gotten hard.

You can't grow where you've gone numb. Tilling means making space for God to breathe fresh life into places that feel stuck, dry, or buried. This part takes time. It requires presence and patience. But without it, the seed won't take root.

DESIGNED TO CULTIVATE

Without tilling, seeds stay on the surface, where birds can snatch them away. Hardened hearts are like untended soil—seeds won't take root. We can plant seeds daily, but without preparing the soil, they won't last. Tilling takes time as we connect and get to know people, but it's a crucial step in nurturing growth.

3. Pull the Rocks and Weeds & Fertilize

Now it's time to get your hands dirty.

- **The rocks** are the burdens and past hurts that harden your heart.
- **The weeds** are the lies you've believed—some so familiar, they almost look like truth.

Weeds often *disguise* themselves as harmless, but over time, they choke out growth. Don't just cut them back—**uproot them**. And when you pull them out, fill the space with truth. That's the fertilizer.

What truths do you need to speak over your heart today? What Scripture will feed the soil of your soul?

When your soil is nourished with truth, growth can finally begin.

4. Plant Seeds

The day you plant the seed is not the day you see the fruit. We carry the seeds of the gospel—truth, love, hope—in our words and our actions. Planting seeds might look like:

- Inviting your neighbor over for dinner
- Checking in on a struggling friend
- Praying with someone who's hurting
- Sharing your testimony, even when it's scary

INTENTIONALLY DESIGNED

Sometimes the seed is a conversation. Sometimes it's a quiet act of kindness. Sometimes it's simply showing up.

As one of my favorite mentors used to say:

"We place truth on their hearts so that when their heart breaks, truth drops in."

You don't have to push or force anything. Just plant. And trust that God knows when the harvest will come.

5. Water the Soil

Growth doesn't happen without water. In a garden, water keeps the soil soft and nourishes the roots. Spiritually, water represents the love, encouragement, truth, and time you invest in people and relationships.

It's the late-night text that says, *I'm still here.*
It's praying for a friend behind the scenes.
It's following up. Listening. Staying consistent.

But here's the beautiful thing: sometimes the rain comes straight from heaven. God sends divine appointments, unexpected breakthroughs, and grace that we could never produce ourselves.

> *"The water that I will give him will become in him a spring of water welling up to eternal life."*
> John 4:14

You water faithfully. God sends the rain. And together, transformation begins.

6. Watch Growth Come Forward

You plant and water. But only God makes things grow.

> *"I planted, Apollos watered, but God gave the growth."*
> 1 Corinthians 3:6

This requires us to depend on God entirely. We give Him our best and let Him do the rest. We give Him the ordinary and let Him do the extraordinary. You reap what you sow, but not always in the timing you hoped for.

Sometimes we don't see the fruit right away. Sometimes it feels like nothing is happening. But God is always working—deep in the soil, behind the scenes. Your job isn't to force the outcome. It's to be faithful.

Even when it's slow. Even when it's quiet. Even when someone else's garden seems to be blooming faster than yours.

God doesn't promise *worldly* fruit, but He does promise fruit of the Spirit:

> "But the fruit of the Spirit is love, joy, peace, patience, kindness, goodness, faithfulness, gentleness, self-control; against such things there is no law."
> Galatians 5:22-23

That's the kind of fruit that really matters. And it lasts forever.

Let's be people who see fruit and growth in others, celebrate it, and bless them. It can be easy to compare their lives to ours, but we must remember we are all on the same team.

7. Trim and Add Structure

Even good fruit needs pruning. Sometimes growth gets heavy, and if it's not supported, it can break the branch. That's where pruning and structure come in.

Pruning might feel like a loss. But in God's hands, it's preparation for more fruit.

INTENTIONALLY DESIGNED

"Every branch that does bear fruit He prunes, that it may bear more fruit."
John 15:2

Structure is the trellis that supports the vine. Spiritually, that means having rhythms and relationships in place that help you grow strong:
- Time in God's Word
- Prayer
- Worship
- Mentorship
- Accountability
- Sabbath
- Serving

These are not boxes to check—they're the framework that helps your life flourish. What works for you in one season might not work for you in another, so we must adjust our structure.

I love how gardens are woven all throughout Scripture. It all started in a garden, where God formed Adam from the dust and gave him purpose.

Jesus prayed in a garden before going to the cross—fully surrendered to His Father's will. And after the resurrection, Mary encountered Him in a garden . . . and mistook Him for the gardener.

"Jesus said to her, "Woman, why are you weeping? Whom are you seeking?" Supposing him to be the gardener, she said to him, "Sir, if you have carried him away, tell me where you have laid him, and I will take him away."
John 20:15

How fitting is that? Mary thought He was the gardener—because He is. Jesus is still tending hearts. Still planting hope. Still pulling weeds and growing fruit and

DESIGNED TO CULTIVATE

calling dead things back to life. And He's doing it in you.

So, let me ask you:

- How's the soil of your heart right now?
- What's growing in your life, and what might need pruning?
- What has God asked you to cultivate in this season?

You don't have to figure it all out. You don't have to do it perfectly, but you do have to show up in the garden. God will meet you there.

Father God,

Thank You for designing me to cultivate—to nurture, grow, and steward the things You've entrusted to me. Whether it's my relationships, my gifts, or the dreams You've planted in my heart, help me to be faithful in tending to them with care and diligence. Teach me to cultivate a life that bears fruit for Your Kingdom, rooted in Your Word and led by Your Spirit.
When I face challenges or seasons of waiting, give me patience and perseverance, knowing that growth takes time. Let me be a faithful steward of what You've given me, always seeking to glorify You in all I do.

In Jesus' name,
Amen.

INTENTIONALLY DESIGNED

Chapter 5: Designed with Needs

Have you ever been called needy? Or maybe nobody said it out loud, but you felt that way? The word needy tends to carry a negative connotation, like it's something to be ashamed of. But here's the truth: needs are not a weakness—they're part of our design. Needs remind us that we're not self-sufficient, and they point us back to the One who is. God created us with needs so that we would rely on Him. When we stop running from our needs and start recognizing them as invitations, our lives can be transformed. Needs aren't flaws to fix—they're a holy reminder that apart from God, we can do nothing. And when we try to meet our needs apart from Him, we end up building idols to fulfill what only He can. It's time to tear those idols down and come back to the Source.

Every single one of us is needy. We each have emotional, physical, spiritual, and relational needs. I have a tattoo on my right arm of a bunch of sparrows. Every time I see it, or I see birds, I am reminded that the God we serve takes care of us. How easy is it to become more focused on our needs than on our provider? It is more common to hear somebody say, "I am so anxious" than it is to hear somebody say, "I have so much peace."

"Therefore I tell you, do not be anxious about your life, what you will eat or what you will drink, nor about your body, what you will put on. Is not life more than food, and the body more than clothing? Look at the birds of the air: they neither sow nor reap nor gather into barns, and yet your heavenly Father feeds them. Are you not of more value than they? And which of you by being

INTENTIONALLY DESIGNED

anxious can add a single hour to his span of life? And why are you anxious about clothing? Consider the lilies of the field, how they grow: they neither toil nor spin, yet I tell you, even Solomon in all his glory was not arrayed like one of these. But if God so clothes the grass of the field, which today is alive and tomorrow is thrown into the oven, will he not much more clothe you, O you of little faith? Therefore do not be anxious, saying, 'What shall we eat?' or 'What shall we drink?' or 'What shall we wear?' For the Gentiles seek after all these things, and your heavenly Father knows that you need them all. But seek first the kingdom of God and his righteousness, and all these things will be added to you. Therefore do not be anxious about tomorrow, for tomorrow will be anxious for itself. Sufficient for the day
is its own trouble."
Matthew 6:25-34

    We have needs—God even acknowledges them—but I'm curious to know if you tend to focus on your needs being fulfilled first or seeking first the kingdom of God? Many of us tell ourselves we seek His kingdom first, but we won't start until we've eaten, drank, or are dressed and ready for the day. Many of us are seeking our own things that are still important, but we've lost sight of what we need to do first. Some of us claim to be seeking God, yet we fail to face Him and gaze at His face. So, for starters, let's look at Jesus.

    Praying differently changed my life. I know there isn't a perfect way to pray. But instead of focusing on what I needed or wanted, I started thanking God for who He is. My husband and I were full-time missionaries for a few years before we were married, and we had to rely on financial support from sponsors. It was so easy for me to focus on the lack of finances that I felt. Instead of saying, "Dear God, I really need more money," I started praying things like, "God, I thank you for being my provider. Thank you for everything you have given me and will give me in

DESIGNED WITH NEEDS

the future. Lord, help me steward well and use patience and self-control." Instead of praying something like, "God, I need healing," I would pray, "Thank you, God, that you are the healer." I began to declare the character and nature of God with a heart of thanksgiving and gratitude. Did I always see a huge abundance? No, but it changed my heart, posture, and perspective. It helped me trust He is who He says He is.

Our needs are an invitation to humility. They push us to stop pretending we have it all together and start depending on the God who holds everything together. Jesus came to earth as a baby—needing to be fed, held, and protected. If even He experienced need, we don't have to be ashamed of ours. We can't escape our needs; they're woven into our DNA.

Every single one of us is a masterpiece. We are God's artwork, His handiwork. We are God's vulnerable expression of His love for the world. God thoughtfully crafted us with needs on purpose.

> "For we are God's handiwork, created in Christ Jesus to do good works, which God prepared in advance for us to do."
> Ephesians 2:10

Jesus came to the Earth with needs. As a baby, He needed someone to feed Him and change His diapers. Jesus needed someone to hold Him, protect Him, and nurture Him—even the Savior of the world, in His humanity, experienced dependence. Yet, the difference is profound: while we are not self-sustaining, God is. He doesn't need anything from us, but He lovingly meets us in our needs.

We are made in the image of God, and part of that design includes having needs—physical, emotional, spiritual, and relational. As Jackie Hill Perry said at IF Gathering in 2020, "Some of us need to be reminded that

INTENTIONALLY DESIGNED

neediness is okay. The problem is when we rebel against God to get a need met. Whether you are trusting an idol for your identity, security, or peace, you are trusting in a dead thing to give you life."[1]

This is the power of the gospel: Jesus, who fully understands what it means to have needs, rose from the grave to meet our greatest need: reconciliation with God. He wasn't left on the cross or in the tomb; He was raised to life to atone for our sins and to give us true, eternal life.

When we recognize our needs and bring them to God, we acknowledge our dependence on Him as the only One who can truly meet them. And when we trust Him to provide, we no longer have to look to idols or dead things for life—we look to the One who is alive forever, meeting our every need in His perfect time.

Let's stop looking to dead things to meet living needs. Let's look at four core areas where we are designed to need—and be met by—the living God.

PHYSICAL NEEDS

Our physical needs include necessities like food, water, clothing, and health. In the Old Testament, after Moses led the Israelites out of slavery in Egypt, they were in the desert and looking for fulfillment of their physical needs. Moses knew if he asked God, He would provide. In Numbers 20:1-11, God provided water from a rock when the Israelites were thirsty. Later, He sent manna from heaven, but their impatience led them to build a golden calf. They craved control more than communion.

Their restless desire for immediate answers led them to idolatry. What's heartbreaking is their fixation on their unmet needs—food, water, and control—blinded them to God's faithfulness and provision. They became so consumed by what they thought they lacked that they forgot to trust the One who could meet every need.

DESIGNED WITH NEEDS

This misplaced focus had a devastating consequence: the majority of the Israelites missed out on the promised land. They let their immediate desires and impatience pull their attention away from God's promises, and as a result, they forfeited the blessings He had prepared for them.

Are we doing the same? Are we so consumed by our needs that we fail to trust God with the bigger picture? Are we chasing temporary comforts, idols, or quick fixes instead of seeking His presence and provision? When we focus solely on our needs, we risk missing out on the abundant life He's calling us to—a life rooted in His promises, purpose, and provision.

That said, acknowledging our needs isn't wrong. God created us as whole beings with physical, emotional, spiritual, and relational needs. When we cultivate these areas that align with His design, we position ourselves to step into the abundant life He has for us fully. For example, our physical needs—like rest, nourishment, and movement—are essential for maintaining the strength and energy to follow Him wholeheartedly.

By cultivating a healthy mind, body, and spirit, we can better steward the life God has entrusted to us and remain focused on His promises rather than distracted by our anxieties. When we approach our needs in faith, we're no longer driven by fear or impatience. Instead, we're living with trust in God, who provides exactly what we need, exactly when we need it.

Here are some practical ways to begin cultivating a healthy mind, body, and spirit:

Practical Tips for Stewarding Physical Health:

- Walking
- Hydration

INTENTIONALLY DESIGNED

- Eating Nourishing Foods
- Rest
- Community

EMOTIONAL NEEDS

If we are emotionally immature, we won't be spiritually mature. The two go hand in hand. Being emotionally mature does not mean we don't experience difficult emotions, but it's what we do with them. I used to believe that as I grew older, I would "have it all together," but it's such a lie. Now, I believe God has everything under control and is holding me. I often think of God as my Dad. Would I climb up into His lap and cry? Would I also share my dreams and passions with Him? We get some great examples from David in the Psalms as he shares lament and praise. Our physical, emotional, and spiritual maturity all align with one another, and when one is out of place, it easily pulls the others out of alignment.

EMOTIONAL RESILIENCE

I remember working at a School of Worship, where a few people were having a tiff among themselves. One of the girls asked if she could leave and spend time with Jesus and return to practice later, and you'll probably be shocked by what I said to her.

I told her no. I told her that right now, she needed to choose to cling to Jesus in the moment and abide in Him, and He would help her right here, right now. There is absolutely a time and place for spending time with Jesus alone. Quiet moments of solitude are essential to refuel and strengthen our relationship with Him. It's in those times we receive personal revelation, peace, and the intimacy that comes from undistracted communion with the Father. But there's another kind of spiritual growth that happens when we face challenges head-on. When we have the opportunity to choose Him in the moment, right in the middle of conflict or discomfort, that's when our faith is truly tested.

A lot of us don't like or want to do hard things. We just want the quiet time, the rest, the affirmation. But when we choose Jesus in the midst of conflict, in front of others, that's when the refining happens. That's when accountability becomes a tool for growth, sharpening us in ways we can't experience in isolation. If we're honest, many of us want to have quiet time with God by ourselves because we've taken offense and want to be affirmed that we were right. However, true growth doesn't come from seeking validation for our feelings—it comes when we allow God to meet us in the hard moments, refining us through accountability and our dependence on Him.

It's in these real-life situations that we learn to trust Him, rely on His strength, and grow into the people He's calling us to be. Quiet time with Jesus is essential, but so is the choice to abide in Him in the middle of life's challenges.

Strategies for Emotional Resilience:

- **Purposefully try something that you don't think you'll be good at.**

Stepping outside your comfort zone and trying new activities, especially those you doubt you'll excel in, fosters a growth mindset. This practice teaches you to embrace failure as a natural part of learning rather than a negative outcome. It helps build resilience by challenging perfectionism and the fear of failure, allowing you to develop a more flexible and positive outlook on challenges. When you allow yourself to engage in activities without the pressure of being perfect, you learn to appreciate the process rather than fixate on the outcome. This flexibility cultivates self-acceptance, reduces anxiety about performance, and enhances your ability to cope with setbacks.

INTENTIONALLY DESIGNED

- **When you feel stuck in your head, move your body.**

Physical activity is a powerful way to break free from negative thought patterns and emotional stagnation. Exercise releases endorphins, which can improve mood and reduce feelings of stress or anxiety. Movement can help shift your focus from overthinking to present-moment awareness, allowing you to process emotions and thoughts more effectively. Engaging in physical activity helps to clear your mind and release pent-up emotions, fostering a sense of empowerment. This practice boosts your mood and helps you regain control over your thoughts and feelings, making you more resilient in challenging situations.

- **Instead of numbing out, allow yourself to feel.**

In moments of stress or discomfort, it's common to want to numb painful feelings through distractions or unhealthy coping mechanisms. Allowing yourself to experience your emotions fully—whether they're positive or negative—promotes emotional awareness and healing. Acknowledging your feelings helps you process them, preventing emotional buildup and promoting a healthier response to adversity. When you allow yourself to feel, you become more attuned to your emotional state and better equipped to handle future challenges. This practice fosters emotional intelligence and helps you understand your triggers, ultimately leading to a more resilient mindset.

- **Practice Self-Care.**

Self-care involves intentionally taking time for activities that nourish your body, mind, and spirit. Prioritizing self-care can prevent burnout, reduce stress, and improve overall well-being. It is essential to recognize that self-care is not selfish; it is a necessary practice for maintaining emotional health and resilience. By practicing self-care, you build a reservoir of emotional strength that helps you navigate life's challenges. Regularly engaging in self-care activities allows you to recharge, thus enabling you to respond to stressors with a clearer mind and a more resilient spirit.

- **Stop saying IF and ask God HOW**

Replacing "if" with "how" shifts your focus from doubt and uncertainty to possibility and action. We ask God for His strategy instead of keeping ourselves in the never-ending thought patterns of worry. Instead of questioning whether something can happen, you explore the steps necessary to achieve it. This shift encourages a proactive mindset and opens the door to faith-driven problem-solving. Replacing "if" with "how" shifts your focus from doubt and uncertainty to possibility and action. Instead of questioning whether something can happen, you explore the steps necessary to achieve it. This shift encourages a proactive mindset and opens the door to faith-driven problem-solving.

- **Celebrate Small Victories**

Acknowledging and celebrating even the smallest achievements fosters a positive mindset and reinforces your progress. This practice helps shift your focus from what you haven't accomplished to what you have, creating a sense of accomplishment and motivation to keep moving forward. Celebrating small victories builds confidence and reinforces a sense of agency, making it easier to tackle bigger challenges. This practice cultivates a positive feedback loop, where recognizing progress boosts your motivation and resilience in the face of adversity.

- **Fail Forward**

Embracing failure as a part of the learning process allows

INTENTIONALLY DESIGNED

you to develop resilience by shifting your perspective on setbacks. Rather than viewing failure as a dead end, consider it a stepping stone to growth and improvement. This mindset encourages you to learn from mistakes and use them as opportunities for development. Failing forward fosters a growth mindset and reduces the fear of failure, enabling you to approach challenges with greater confidence. Recognizing that setbacks can lead to valuable lessons empowers you to persist through difficulties and continue striving for success.

SPIRITUAL NEEDS

We all have a deep spiritual need to connect with God. This connection goes beyond the surface level of religious practices and rituals—it's about truly knowing and experiencing Him. The spirit of religion has often robbed us of this intimacy by reducing our relationship with God to a checklist of rules and obligations, but God desires more for us. He wants us to experience Him in a real, tangible way, not just intellectually but emotionally and spiritually.

Connecting with God isn't just about knowing the Bible or memorizing Scripture, although those are valuable. It's about encountering His presence, hearing His voice, and allowing His love to transform us from the inside out.

If we look at the life of Jesus, we see the perfect example of someone who lived in deep, continuous connection with the Father. Even though He was fully God, Jesus demonstrated He had spiritual needs as a man on Earth. He regularly withdrew to be alone with the Father, showing us the importance of silence and solitude in cultivating that connection.

Mark 1:35: "Very early in the morning, while it was still dark, Jesus got up, left the house and went off to a solitary place, where He prayed." After an exhausting day of healing and teaching, Jesus still chose to rise early and seek the Father's presence.

Luke 6:12: Before selecting His disciples, Jesus spent the entire night in prayer, seeking the Father's guidance for this pivotal decision.

Matthew 14:23: After feeding the 5,000, Jesus dismissed the crowds and went up on a mountainside by Himself to pray. Even after a great miracle, He sought renewal from the Father.

Matthew 26:36-39: In the Garden of Gethsemane, Jesus poured out His heart in anguish, seeking strength and alignment with God's will before facing the cross.

These moments weren't just about checking a spiritual box; they were about communion, alignment, and renewal. Jesus modeled that time with the Father isn't optional—it's essential.

Practices for Spiritual Growth

Silence & Solitude

Silence and solitude are spiritual practices that help us meet this need for connection with God. In the busyness of life, it's easy to get swept up in distractions and lose sight of our spiritual needs. But Jesus invites us to pause, step away from the noise, and be with Him.

1. Silence. This is where we quiet the external and internal noise to hear God's voice. Silence allows us to move past the clutter of our thoughts and tune into His presence.

2. Solitude. Solitude isn't just being alone; it's being alone with God. In solitude, we reflect, pray, and listen,

INTENTIONALLY DESIGNED

creating space for God to speak and refresh our spirits.

Prayer

Prayer is an essential practice that allows for open communication with God. There isn't a formula to it. Prayer is simply talking to God throughout the day. It provides a space for you to express your thoughts, seek guidance, and pour out your heart to Him. Through prayer, you develop intimacy with God and learn to rely on His strength and wisdom in all aspects of life. Regular prayer deepens your relationship with God and fosters a sense of trust in His plans. It also helps you discern His will, guiding your decisions and actions. As you grow in your prayer life, you develop a deeper understanding of God's character, leading to increased faith and spiritual maturity.

Tips to Incorporate Prayer In Your Life:

1. Start your day with a simple prayer like, "God, guide me today."
2. Use short prayers throughout the day: "Help me with this task" or "Thank You for this moment."
3. Before bed, reflect on your day and thank God for His blessings.

Meditating on the Word

Meditation on Scripture involves reflecting on and internalizing God's Word. This practice allows you to draw strength and wisdom from biblical truths, transforming your understanding of God's promises and how they apply to your life. Meditating on the Word helps you internalize God's truth, leading to a transformed mindset and a deeper understanding of His ways. As you engage with Scripture, you grow in wisdom, knowledge, and spiritual discernment, which can shape your beliefs and actions in alignment with God's will.

DESIGNED WITH NEEDS

Tips to Focus on God's Word:

1. Choose one Bible verse and write it on a sticky note to keep with you all day.
2. Spend five minutes in silence, thinking about what the verse means for your life.
3. Use an app or devotional guide to help you dig deeper into a chapter each week.

WORSHIP

Worship is an expression of love and reverence toward God, encompassing various forms, such as singing, prayer, and acts of service. It shifts your focus from your circumstances to God's greatness and character, fostering a deeper appreciation for His love and sovereignty. Worship allows you to experience God's presence and cultivate a heart of gratitude and praise. This practice deepens your connection with God and encourages you to align your life with His purposes. Through worship, you can gain insights into His character and your identity in Him, fostering spiritual growth and maturity.

Tips to Incorporate Worship In Your Life:

1. Play a worship song while driving and sing along.
2. Write a list of things you're thankful for and turn it into a prayer of gratitude.
3. Serve someone in need as an act of worship, reflecting God's love through your actions.

MENTORSHIP

Having a mentor in your spiritual journey provides guidance, support, and accountability. A mentor can share their experiences, offer wisdom, and help you navigate challenges in your faith journey, encouraging you to grow in your understanding of God and His Word. Mentorship fosters spiritual growth by providing opportunities for

INTENTIONALLY DESIGNED

learning and reflection. A mentor can challenge you to deepen your faith, explore new spiritual practices, and hold you accountable in your walk with God. This relationship encourages you to grow in wisdom and discernment, guiding you toward greater spiritual maturity.

Tips For Mentorship:

1. Ask a trusted friend or church leader to meet for coffee once a month.
2. Be open about areas where you need encouragement or advice.
3. Reflect on what you've learned from your mentor and apply it in your daily life.

RELATIONAL NEEDS

We know we're designed for community. We believe we are connected through technology, but most of us aren't truly known and loved for who we are. Some of us have been told lies that we are too much or not enough. People pleasing doesn't serve anybody. You can't serve two masters.

"No one can serve two masters. Either you will hate the one and love the other, or you will be devoted to the one and despise the other."
Matthew 6:24

Having relationships is a need. If babies are left alone without touch, they will die. We need each other now more than ever. I love looking at relationships in scripture to encourage us in the pursuit of community. Let's look at Ruth & Naomi.

Ruth and Naomi both had a heart for God, which is what they bonded over. Some people would rather bond over trauma or gossip instead of bonding over the glory of God. Our relationships should be built on the foundation

DESIGNED WITH NEEDS

of love for God. Ruth was Naomi's daughter-in-law. They weren't just two friends who were the same age and in the same season of life. Naomi moved to Moab due to a famine. Her husband, Elimelech, and her two sons died, leaving her with her daughters-in-law, one of them being Ruth. Naomi decided to go back to Bethlehem after the death of her loved ones and encouraged her daughters-in-law to return to their own families, but Ruth refused to leave Naomi by herself.

"But Ruth said, "Do not urge me to leave you or to return from following you. For where you go I will go, and where you lodge I will lodge. Your people shall be my people, and your God my God. Where you die I will die, and there will I be buried. May the Lord do so to me and more also if anything but death parts me from you."
Ruth 1:16-17

Ruth expressed deep loyalty and love to Naomi, committing to stay by her side no matter the circumstances. They returned to Bethlehem together, a beautiful example of God's provision through relationships. In Bethlehem, they faced poverty, and Ruth took on the humble task of working in the fields, gathering leftover grain to provide for both of them. In these fields, she caught the attention of a man named Boaz, who was not only related to Naomi but also a man of great character and integrity. Boaz, moved by Ruth's faithfulness, made sure they had enough food and protection, ensuring their safety among the workers. Eventually, Ruth married Boaz, and he provided a secure future for both her and Naomi, redeeming their story. I love how God can meet needs through people, working through relationships to bring restoration and provision at just the right time.

Tips to Nurture Relationships

1. Show up for your people
2. Make your friends a meal

INTENTIONALLY DESIGNED

3. Call them on your way to work
4. Listen to their joys and sorrow
5. Send an encouraging text
6. Pray for them
7. Dream with them
8. Root for them

Instead of looking at our needs as a weakness or our identity, let's look to our Heavenly Father, who meets all our needs. Let's have a heart of thanksgiving and gratitude, and remember that He will take care of us.

Your needs are not a curse. They are a call—to depend on God, to connect with others, and to grow in grace. Stop seeing your needs as something to hide. Start seeing them as something that points you back to your Father.

Heavenly Father,

Thank You for creating me with needs that draw me closer to You. Help me to recognize that my deepest longings and desires are met fully in Your love and presence. Teach me to trust in Your provision and care, and remind me that I am not my weakness but that Your power is made PERFECT in my weakness. You've designed me to depend on You. May I seek You first in all things, trusting that You know what I need even before I ask.

In Jesus' name,
Amen.

Chapter 6:
Designed with Purpose

Our purpose is the compass of our lives. What is a compass? A compass tells you where you are going. Each of us has a unique, intentional purpose—a calling from God to live with focus, passion, and direction. Maybe you're reading this and thinking, *I'm not sure what mine is.* That's okay. You're not behind. You're not too late. Let's unpack this together.

We often complicate the idea of purpose, layering it with pressure, comparison, and fear. The world hands us a roadmap filled with titles, timelines, and milestones, but Scripture gives us something simpler and far more powerful: **your purpose is to glorify God**. That's it. Your life, your words, your gifts—they were designed to shine the light of Jesus so others might see Him through you.

But so many of us feel stuck, and when we feel stuck, we feel purposeless. Here are a few common roadblocks:

- Believing our past disqualifies us
- Not feeling qualified or equipped
- Fear of starting small
- Uncertainty about our giftings
- Apathy or spiritual burnout
- Lack of support or encouragement
- Difficulty discerning God's voice

The truth is: you are already commissioned. Ephesians 2:10 says you are God's workmanship, created for good works which He prepared in advance for you to do. That means you're not waiting to be called—you already are. If God has called you to it, He will see you through it. Don't let fear hold you back. Don't let finances hold you back. If it's God's will, it's God's bill, amen?

Purpose doesn't pause; it pivots. Our purpose itself doesn't change—our ultimate calling is to glorify God with our lives. But how we live that out can shift depending on the season we're in, the opportunities God places before us, or even the challenges we face. New seasons bring new assignments. Your purpose may shift from leading a ministry to leading your children. From a stage to a kitchen table. From building your dream to helping someone else build theirs. In those moments, it can feel like the forward momentum of purpose has come to a halt. But here's the truth: God is never idle, and neither is the purpose He's given you. It's all purposeful when it's all for His glory.

The pivot doesn't mean you've lost your purpose. It means you're aligning with God's plan for this moment. What pivots is *how* we do that with our lives. When it comes to discovering how to live out that purpose practically, ask yourself:

- What are my strengths?
- Where am I weak, and where could God show up in that?
- What am I passionate about?
- What makes me come alive?

We tend to wait for big clarity before we move, but God often gives us one next step. Our job is not to figure it all out—our job is obedience. We do our best. God handles the rest.

In Matthew 28, Jesus gives the Great Commission—not just to missionaries, but to all believers: Go and make disciples. Whether that's across the world or across your street, your mission is people. Not places. Your purpose is active, not passive. So why are we so often tempted to sit on the sidelines?

DESIGNED WITH PURPOSE

"Now the eleven disciples went to Galilee, to the mountain to which Jesus had directed them. And when they saw him they worshiped him, but some doubted. And Jesus came and said to them, "All authority in heaven and on earth has been given to me. Go therefore and make disciples of all nations, baptizing them in the name of the Father and of the Son and of the Holy Spirit, teaching them to observe all that I have commanded you. And behold, I am with you always, to the end of the age."
Matthew 28:16-20

We are called to live with purpose, intentionally and boldly. Jesus gave His life for you—so will you live for Him? Why have so many of us grown content to let others do the work while we simply sit back and observe? Too often, we've shifted from being active participants in God's mission to passive consumers, forgetting that we are called to be doers of the Word, not merely hearers.

I learned this firsthand on a mission trip to Bali, Indonesia—one of my favorite places in the world. During one visit, I got into a motorbike accident. My helmet hit the pavement, my arm was injured, and I was left shaken and physically hurting. But three days later, I went to church. And there, a little girl—just three years old—came up to me and said, "Jesus told me He wanted to heal somebody today. Can I pray for you?"

Her faith stunned me. She didn't wait for permission, affirmation, or a perfect plan. She simply obeyed.

That little girl's simple obedience unlocked something in me—not just physical healing, but spiritual and emotional healing. Her father later told me, "God wants you to ask Him where He was in the middle of your accident." When I did, I saw a beam of light—a holy presence—go before me in the moment of my crash. God spoke to my heart: *"I went before you. I always will. I took*

INTENTIONALLY DESIGNED

the hit for you on the cross—and I always will."

That moment changed everything. All because a child said yes.

We don't need to wait until we feel ready to be obedient. Jess Connolly once said, "Some of us are trying so hard to be obedient that we are being disobedient."[2] Too often, we overthink obedience. Sometimes our delay—under the guise of preparation—is really just fear. But Scripture reminds us: we live by faith, not by sight (2 Corinthians 5:7).

That little girl didn't live by sight; she lived by faith. She showed up, prayed boldly, and let God do the rest. Her faith brought healing to my life in ways I didn't even know I needed.

So, what about you? Where is God asking you to step out in faith today? What act of obedience is He calling you to that might bring healing—not just to you, but to someone else? Don't wait to feel ready. Trust Him and go.

Faith leads to obedience. Abraham is a perfect example.

In Genesis 12, God called Abraham to leave everything he knew with one promise: *"I will show you."* Abraham didn't receive the whole picture, but he went. Hebrews 11:8 says, "By faith Abraham obeyed." Faith wasn't passive. It moved.

Abraham's story also shows us what happens when we doubt. God promised Abraham a son, but in fear and impatience, Abraham took control and had Ishmael, born out of disobedience. And yet, even in that detour, God was faithful. Isaac—the child of promise—was born, and Abraham's obedience in later years (even to the point of almost sacrificing Isaac) showed deep trust in God's character.

"By faith Abraham obeyed when he was called to go out to a place that he was to receive as an inheritance. And he went out, not knowing where he was going. 9 By faith he went to live in the land of promise, as in a foreign land, living in tents with Isaac and Jacob, heirs with him of the same promise."
Hebrews 11:8-9

So what holds us back from obedience?

1. **Doubt** – "Did God really say...?"
2. **Disqualification** – "I'm not ready. I'm not enough."
3. **Idolatry of Calling** – We worship the calling more than the One who called us.

Here's the good news: God doesn't call the qualified—He qualifies the called. If He can use a three-year-old girl in Bali, He can use you. As we reflected on earlier, 2 Corinthians 12:9 reminds us His power is made perfect in our weakness, so stop disqualifying yourself from the work God is asking you to do.

When we chase calling more than Christ, we get exhausted, but when we follow Christ, He leads us into our calling naturally. Mark 10:39 says whoever loses their life for Christ will find it. When we surrender our striving, we find the peace and clarity we've been searching for.

How do we make this shift from striving and chasing after the "perfect" calling to living in the fullness of God's purpose for us? It begins with surrender. Rather than seeking external measures of success, we start by surrendering our desires, our plans, and our idea of "perfection" to God. When we stop trying to control the outcomes and instead let Him guide our steps, we discover that He is more than enough—His purpose for us

INTENTIONALLY DESIGNED

is more than we could ever chase down on our own.

So what do you do with all of this?

- **Worship God with your whole life** – Whether it's small or big, let it bring Him glory (1 Corinthians 10:31).
- **Let your works be the overflow** – Don't serve to earn. Serve because you've already been loved.
- **Put faith into action** – James 2:14-16 shows us that faith without works is dead. True belief shows up in how we live.

Obedience isn't optional. It's the natural response to a heart transformed by Jesus. If our faith isn't moving us, is it really faith at all?

> "Dear friends, do you think you'll get anywhere in this if you learn all the right words but never do anything? Does merely talking about faith indicate that a person really has it? For instance, you come upon an old friend dressed in rags and half-starved and say, "Good morning, friend! Be clothed in Christ! Be filled with the Holy Spirit!" and walk off without providing so much as a coat or a cup of soup—where does that get you? Isn't it obvious that God-talk without God-acts is outrageous nonsense? I can already hear one of you agreeing by saying, "Sounds good. You take care of the faith department, I'll handle the works department." Not so fast. You can no more show me your works apart from your faith than I can show you my faith apart from my works. Faith and works, works and faith, fit together hand in glove."
> James 2:14-16

I love the Message version of this verse. Walk into the room like God sent you there. Walk like the same power that raised Jesus from the grave is inside of you. The Holy Spirit is with you. It is a gift given to us because Jesus himself

DESIGNED WITH PURPOSE

said it would be better this way. God gives good gifts that glorify him.

Picture this: I ask my daughter Denver to clean her room. She replies, "I'm going to pray about it, listen to a podcast, and talk to my friends first." Sounds ridiculous, right? But how often do we do the same with God's simple instructions?

Luke 16:10 says if we're faithful in the small, we'll be trusted with much. So start small. Start now.

THE ECHO OF ETERNITY

If we were obedient to the Holy Spirit, this world would be a different place. I don't know about you, but I love Dr. Pepper. You know that moment when you crack open a can, and you hear that satisfying fizz as the carbonation rises to the top? It's full of energy, full of life—just for a split second. Then, just like that, it settles. The bubbles disappear, and that moment is gone. You almost wonder where it went.

That fizz—just like life—is so quick. The Bible says this life is but a vapor, a mist that appears for a little while and then vanishes (James 4:14). Think about it: one moment the fizz is there, and the next it's gone. Just like our time here on earth. No matter how long we live, in the grand scheme of eternity, it's brief. That's why it's so important to ask ourselves: *What am I doing with the time I have?*

Are we going to let this vapor of life pass by without being obedient to the call God has placed on us? The fizz might disappear in an instant, but the impact of our choices—our obedience to the Holy Spirit—can echo into eternity. If we live in a way that is focused on God's purpose, on His will, even the shortest of lives can have eternal significance. Just like the fizz that's there for a moment and then vanishes, we have one shot at living

INTENTIONALLY DESIGNED

this life in obedience to God. Let's make it count, because it really is here and then gone. What will we leave behind when the vapor of our life disappears?

I want you to take a moment and reflect with God. If you need to repent and say you are sorry to God, it's always the best time to get right with Him. I'd love for you to share with someone and have them pray for boldness in your obedience to whatever it is that the Holy Spirit asks you to do. Amen?

Questions to Ask Yourself:
1. What is stopping me from being obedient?
2. What is the Holy Spirit asking me to do?
3. Where can I let God show up in my weakness?
4. What do I need to do to be obedient today?
5. Who can hold me accountable/pray with me?

Lord,

Thank You for designing me with a unique and intentional purpose. When I doubt my worth or wonder why I'm here, remind me that You created me with a mission only I can fulfill. Help me to walk boldly in the path You have set before me, knowing that every step is part of Your greater plan. Give me the courage to live out my purpose for Your glory, and may my life reflect the beauty of Your design.

In Jesus' name,
Amen.

Chapter 7:
Designed with Gifts

What is your favorite gift you've ever received? For my 27th birthday, I got so many pink clothing items, which was special because I am OBSESSED with the color pink. If you know me in person or follow my social media, you will see me wearing pink all the time and hear how God redeemed a lot of my life by wearing that color.

It would be ironic to get a gift and never use it. That's what gifts are for, right? How many of us have gotten a gift from someone and hoped there was a gift receipt? Some gifts end up in the donation pile or at a garage sale because we don't fully appreciate or use them for their intended purpose.

The gospel is a gift many of us accept but fail to appreciate fully. Just like that sweater you might never wear, some of us accept the salvation that Jesus offers, but we don't take full advantage of the power and life-restoration that comes with it. The gospel is not just about being saved—it's about the Kingdom of God being established here on earth through the life, death, and resurrection of Jesus. It's a kingdom of abundance, freedom, peace, and the restoration of everything God originally designed in Eden. When Jesus preached the gospel, healings, miracles, and restoration followed. Why? Because the gospel isn't just a "get out of hell free card"— it's a call to live in the fullness of God's plan for our lives right now.

When Jesus went to the cross, He didn't just secure salvation for us; He secured the restoration of everything

INTENTIONALLY DESIGNED

that was lost. How many of us have forgotten that the gospel is not only about salvation but about being restored to the abundant life God always intended for us? It's like receiving a gift and leaving it wrapped up, never fully experiencing its power. The power of God is available to us, not just for eternity, but for today, as we walk in the fullness of His Kingdom.

Jesus has given us the ultimate gift. The question is: Are we using it to its full potential? Are we allowing the gospel to restore our lives, relationships, and purpose the way God intended? The gospel is not meant to sit on a shelf; it's meant to transform us from the inside out, giving us the power to live in abundance and freedom now, not just waiting for heaven. Let's not just accept the gift of salvation—let's embrace the fullness of the life-restoring power of the gospel.

> *"Who has believed what he has heard from us? And to whom has the arm of the Lord been revealed? For he grew up before him like a young plant, and like a root out of dry ground; he had no form or majesty that we should look at him, and no beauty that we should desire him. He was despised and rejected by men, a man of sorrows and acquainted with grief; and as one from whom men hide their faces he was despised, and we esteemed him not. Surely he has borne our griefs and carried our sorrows; yet we esteemed him stricken, smitten by God, and afflicted. But he was pierced for our transgressions; he was crushed for our iniquities; upon him was the chastisement that brought us peace, and with his wounds we are healed."*
> Isaiah 53:1-5

Jesus died on the cross so you can be healed. Jesus's kingdom is a kingdom of power. God's plan A for your life is not oppression or suffering. Jesus gave us the gift of the Holy Spirit to stay connected to God. He gave us the gift of the Holy Spirit so that we can bless others.

DESIGNED WITH GIFTS

"Bless the Lord, O my soul, and all that is within me, bless his holy name!
Bless the Lord, O my soul, and forget not all his benefits, who forgives all your iniquity, who heals all your diseases, who redeems your life from the pit, who crowns you with steadfast love and mercy, who satisfies you with good so that your youth is renewed like the eagle's."
Psalm 103:1-5

If there weren't benefits, why would we follow Him? He forgives us. He saves us. He heals us. He gives us peace. He crowns us with steadfast love and mercy when He pulls us out of the pit. He satisfies us with good and renews us like the youth of an eagle. There are so many blessings/benefits in the kingdom of God, but none of them would be possible without His power.

He has given us the most precious gift of all: the Holy Spirit. Have you ever thought of the Holy Spirit as a gift? It's easy to overlook, but God made a way for Himself to be with us at all times—His presence is alive within us. His power is made perfect in our weaknesses, and this is not a passive gift. It's an active presence that equips us, strengthens us, and empowers us to live out His purpose for our lives.

God doesn't give gifts haphazardly. He gives good gifts. The spiritual gifts He bestows upon us are a reflection of His creativity, love, and His desire for us to participate in His redemptive work here on earth. These gifts are not just for us to admire or keep to ourselves—they are meant to serve a greater purpose. **Our gifts are a testament to God's creativity and His desire for us to participate in His redemptive work.**

Each of us has unique gifts, talents, and abilities specifically designed by our Maker. These gifts are not random—they are intentional, tailored to who we are and

INTENTIONALLY DESIGNED

how God has wired us. They are a part of His design for us to build up His Kingdom and bring glory to His name.

But how do we use these gifts if we don't even know what they are? Just like receiving a thoughtful gift, we must recognize, nurture, and utilize the spiritual gifts God has given us. To fully embrace our calling, we must first become aware of these gifts, ask the Holy Spirit to reveal them, and step out in faith to use them in service to God and others.

The Apostle Paul speaks about spiritual gifts in his letters to the early church.

> "Now concerning spiritual gifts, brothers, I do not want you to be uninformed. You know that when you were pagans you were led astray to mute idols, however you were led. Therefore I want you to understand that no one speaking in the Spirit of God ever says "Jesus is accursed!" and no one can say "Jesus is Lord" except in the Holy Spirit. Now there are varieties of gifts, but the same Spirit; and there are varieties of service, but the same Lord; and there are varieties of activities, but it is the same God who empowers them all in everyone. To each is given the manifestation of the Spirit for the common good. For to one is given through the Spirit the utterance of wisdom, and to another the utterance of knowledge according to the same Spirit, to another faith by the same Spirit, to another gifts of healing by the one Spirit, to another the working of miracles, to another prophecy, to another the ability to distinguish between spirits, to another various kinds of tongues, to another the interpretation of tongues. All these are empowered by one and the same Spirit, who apportions to each one individually as he wills."
> 1 Corinthians 12:1-11

The Gifts:
- Wisdom

DESIGNED WITH GIFTS

- Knowledge
- Faith
- Healing
- Miracles
- Prophecy
- Discernment
- Tongues
- Interpreting Tongues

These gifts are given for the common good and to build up the body of Christ for the glory of God. It clearly states above that even though there are a variety of gifts, it is the same spirit. It is God who empowers the gifts in you. God gives gifts individually as HE WILLS to people.

I love that God doesn't give everybody the same gift. God is a God of diversity, which shows us more of His nature and character through His children. All of the gifts are essential for the church to flourish. We are the body of Christ.

Jesus had twelve disciples, each with a unique story. Fishermen, tax collectors, zealots, and others brought different strengths and perspectives. Having differences didn't hinder the spread of their ministry, but their variation strengthened the disciples by allowing them to reach various people groups to spread the good news of the gospel effectively.

"There is one body, but it has many parts. But all its many parts make up one body. It is the same with Christ. We were all baptized by one Holy Spirit. And so we are formed into one body. It didn't matter whether we were Jews or Gentiles, slaves or free people. We were all given the same Spirit to drink. So the body is not made up of just one part. It has many parts. Suppose the foot says, "I am not a hand. So I don't belong to the body." By saying this, it cannot stop being part of the body. And suppose the ear says, "I am not an eye. So I don't belong to the body." By saying this, it cannot stop

INTENTIONALLY DESIGNED

being part of the body. If the whole body were an eye, how could it hear? If the whole body were an ear, how could it smell? God has placed each part in the body just as he wanted it to be. If all the parts were the same, how could there be a body? As it is, there are many parts. But there is only one body. The eye can't say to the hand, "I don't need you!" The head can't say to the feet, "I don't need you!" In fact, it is just the opposite. The parts of the body that seem to be weaker are the ones we can't do without. The parts that we think are less important we treat with special honor. The private parts aren't shown. But they are treated with special care. The parts that can be shown don't need special care. But God has put together all the parts of the body. And he has given more honor to the parts that didn't have any. In that way, the parts of the body will not take sides. All of them will take care of one another. If one part suffers, every part suffers with it. If one part is honored, every part shares in its joy. You are the body of Christ. Each one of you is a part of it."
1 Corinthians 12:12-27

We are all a part of the body of Christ. God has given us good gifts to use, and if we don't put them into action, it affects the rest of the body. Matthew 25 talks about the parable of the talents; go ahead and read it if you have never read it before. In this story, a master entrusts his servants with varying amounts of talent (currency). The servant who invests his talent is applauded, and the one who buries his talent is rebuked. This parable challenges us to remember to steward the gifts God has given us. Some of us have never even opened the gift, or some may hide their gifts out of fear of what people will think, or because we simply don't want to use them.

Jesus promises us His power through the Holy Spirit, empowering us to use our gifts boldly and purposefully.

"But you will receive power when the Holy Spirit has

DESIGNED WITH GIFTS

come upon you, and you will be my witnesses in Jerusalem and in all Judea and Samaria, and to the end of the earth."
Acts 1:8

This promise was fulfilled at Pentecost when the disciples were filled with the Holy Spirit and began to speak in tongues, proclaiming the mighty works of God to people from various nations. The Holy Spirit doesn't just empower us but also guides us in using our gifts effectively. As we walk in step with the Holy Spirit, we can discern how to use our gifts to align with God's will and bring Him glory.

Maybe you've never fully experienced or recognized the gift God has given you. Perhaps you've prayed over others—or been prayed for—and haven't seen the results you hoped for. That's where the beauty of community comes in. When others come alongside you, praying for you, encouraging you, and sharing their faith with you, they help you step into the gifts God has placed in you. God's Word remains unchanging, and so does His character. He has uniquely designed you with specific gifts to use for His kingdom, and His plan for your life is to empower you to fulfill your purpose. When you choose to make Jesus the Lord of your life and ask for forgiveness, you become part of His family and part of His redemptive work in the world. God's Word is true—yesterday, today, and forever. It doesn't shift with our circumstances, and we need to hold on to that truth, declaring it over our lives and stepping boldly into the gifts He has given us, no matter what we face.

Our gifts aren't for personal gain but to serve others. As we look at the life of Jesus, we see that He was a servant. We see this in the act of Jesus washing His disciples' feet. Jesus said He didn't come to be served but to serve. Our gifts are just a part of us serving others. When we use our gifts to serve others, we reflect the heart of Jesus and get

INTENTIONALLY DESIGNED

to be a part of the work of the Kingdom of God. Service isn't just for church; it's for our families, friends, neighbors, communities, and enemies. Every time we operate in the gifts of the Holy Spirit, it is a manifestation of God's Kingdom on Earth.

So, how do we discover the gift God has given us? This can be a journey. Here are some practical things to do to discover your giftings:

1. **Pray and Reflect.** Seek God in prayer. Tell Him you want to experience Him in His power. Ask Him to reveal the gifts He has placed inside you. Take time to reflect on your passions, strengths, and activities that bring you joy.

2. **Study Scripture.** Read passages that talk about spiritual gifts: 1 Corinthians 12, Romans 12, Ephesians 4. When we understand the Biblical foundation for spiritual giftings, it can help us discern what gifts we have.

3. **Ask For Feedback.** I don't know how many times it's happened that other people see something in me that I don't. Ask trusted friends, mentors, family members, and church leaders to share what giftings they see in you, and ask them to pray for you.

4. **Serve in Ministry.** Serving is where our giftings come alive, so serve in different capacities and see what happens. What is God prompting you to do in those times and places?

5. **Spiritual Gifts Assessment.** These assessments are a great tool to get you started. Your answers may shock you or make perfect sense. You are not limited to the assessment. I also try to take an assessment every few years as the seasons of

DESIGNED WITH GIFTS

my life change. Here's one you can check out: https://gifts.churchgrowth.org/spiritual-gifts-survey/gifts-survey/

6. **Observe the Needs Around You.** Pay attention to the needs in the world around you. What's happening in your church and community? Where are you feeling an urgency or strong sense of compassion to help? God often aligns our hearts with His plans to serve His people.

So, what gift does God want to empower through you as you partner with the Holy Spirit for the common good of others and to build up His church? Are you afraid to show up and use your gifts for the glory of God? Let's do it regardless, even if we're afraid. We choose fear of the Lord over fear of man, in Jesus' name. The world needs the beam of hope that you carry: Jesus. You weren't made to show up small; you were designed to show up in the fullness of who God created you to be.

Being designed with gifts is part of our identity in Christ. As we discover and embrace these gifts, we become active participants in God's plan of redemption and restoration. In this new Kingdom, He established that our gifts are not just abilities to be admired but tools to be used out of the overflow of our relationship with God for His glory and for the goodness of others. May we seek the Lord on the gifts He has intentionally given, cultivate them with excellence and humility, and use them to shine the light of God's glory in a world that needs it. By using our gifts, we will walk in our God-given design and help Heaven come to Earth.

"And let us not grow weary of doing good, for in due season we will reap, if we do not give up."
Galatians 6:9

INTENTIONALLY DESIGNED

Father,

You are the Giver of every good and perfect gift, and I thank You for the unique talents and abilities You've placed within me. Help me use these gifts not for my glory, but to serve others and advance Your Kingdom. When I feel inadequate or compare myself to others, remind me that You have given me everything I need to fulfill my calling. Help me to steward these gifts with humility and faithfulness.

In Jesus' name,
Amen.

Chapter 8: Designed to Create

Co-creation is a beautiful partnership between humanity and the Trinity. When God created everything, it was a partnership. God thought it, Jesus spoke it, and the Holy Spirit made it happen. That's not just a catchy phrase—it's the blueprint of creation and the rhythm of how God still moves today. In Genesis 1, we see the Father's perfect design.

> *"In the beginning, **God created** the heavens and the earth... and the Spirit of God was hovering over the waters."*
> Genesis 1:1–2

God *thought* it. He envisioned the world and all of creation before it even began to take shape. Then, in verse 3, God said, "Let there be light," and there was light. Jesus, the Word made flesh, *spoke* creation into existence.

> *"In the beginning was the Word, and the Word was with God, and the Word was God."*
> John 1:1

The Holy Spirit, who was present from the very start, took the Word and *activated* it.

> *"And if the Spirit of Him who raised Jesus from the dead is living in you, He will also give life to your mortal bodies."*
> Romans 8:11

That same Spirit still brings life today—activating the Word of God in our hearts and enabling us to live out

INTENTIONALLY DESIGNED

the purpose He designed for us.

It's a dynamic relationship where we, as God's children, are invited to participate in His ongoing creative work. This partnership started in the garden. From the beginning, God showed us His desire for partnership. In Genesis, we read about how He created the world and then invited Adam to name the animals, an act of co-creation that highlighted humanity's role in God's plan and showed His heart for us. I imagine my kids and the imaginations they have when they draw a picture and tell me what it is. Let's explore what it means to co-create with God, how we can embrace this calling, and the transformative impact it can have on our lives and the world around us.

God's creative nature is evident throughout Scripture. He is the ultimate Creator, crafting the universe with intricate detail and profound beauty. As His image-bearers, we are given the ability and calling to create alongside Him.

In the Bible, we find numerous examples of co-creation. Noah built the ark following God's precise instructions. God gave him measurements, and Noah put in the work. Noah's co-creating with God protected his family and quite a few animals! Bezalel and Oholiab were filled with the Spirit of God to craft the Tabernacle. The Tabernacle was a sacred place for the Lord to dwell, where only the chosen few were allowed in. Co-creation involves hearing God's voice, receiving His guidance, and utilizing our unique skills to bring His vision to life.

When I was a senior in high school, I remember sitting at school and hearing Buck Bloggett share about the Love > Hate Project. His daughter had been murdered by an ex-boyfriend. She had been in an orchestra with me, and I remember buying a CD she recorded of her own songs. She was one of the sweetest people.

DESIGNED TO CREATE

I felt a stirring in me to do something. Buck talked about how love is the answer to fighting hate. That night, at my youth group, I heard Brian Hunter preach about running across Mongolia. He did it for the kids who had to sleep in the sewer next to the pipes to try to keep warm. My heart felt so much compassion.

I've found that when my heart feels compassion, action is the next step. I drove home with my friend Holly, and I remember telling her in the pickup truck, "I think God wants me to run across Wisconsin to raise awareness about human trafficking." I had to do something.

I told my parents, and they were on board with one condition: my dad would be the one to train me for the run. I began praying daily about what I was supposed to do. The plan was to run from the top of Wisconsin–the city of Superior–down to Milwaukee.

I told myself that if I could run twenty miles a day, then everybody else could do the other twenty miles to cover it for me. I shared my idea with my youth pastor, Jon, and he supported me.

I started selling t-shirts in the lobby at church. They created a promo video for me, and we hosted a Q&A panel to get people on board. As I trained and prayed, God took two of my passions and put them together to fight for freedom—running and human trafficking.

I remember training for six and a half months for this run. Many people supported me, but some thought I was crazy. Some who thought I could have a lifelong injury and those who doubted that God would ever ask a young girl like me to do something like that. But I kept showing up to run and train. God kept providing. He provided my shoes for big miles, our hotel rooms, our groceries, beef sticks for protein on the go, and people who knew how to get the knots out of my muscles. God was there in the

INTENTIONALLY DESIGNED

midst of it all. He brought in support.

My church and community rallied around me. Some joined us in running, some cooked meals, some helped us stretch out all the knots, and some helped us promote it. Our team was united. We started every day with a morning devotional to stay focused. We laughed and cried together. My mom often drove her minivan alongside us while running and would blast music like "You Can't Stop Me" by Andy Mineo. One time, she blasted a Christmas song in the middle of June that made us laugh. While we ran, we would pray and sometimes play a game to keep us going. We played a popcorn story game, where one person would start the story by saying "pop," and then someone else would continue it. We needed those moments of laughter to keep going.

God called me to shed light on a very dark thing still happening in our world. Sometimes, we feel like God asks us to do something that doesn't make sense. I've often felt misunderstood in my pursuit of God, but I have to remember that I fear God more than I fear man. Maybe we feel like it is so far beyond us; maybe we feel incapable. But God can take what little we have and multiply it. **God likes to take what's ordinary and make it extraordinary.**

"After this, Jesus crossed over to the far side of the Sea of Galilee, also known as the Sea of Tiberias. A huge crowd kept following him wherever he went, because they saw his miraculous signs as he healed the sick. Then Jesus climbed a hill and sat down with his disciples around him. (It was nearly time for the Jewish Passover celebration.) Jesus soon saw a huge crowd of people coming to look for him. Turning to Philip, he asked, "Where can we buy bread to feed all these people?" He was testing Philip, for he already knew what he was going to do. Philip replied, "Even if we worked for months, we wouldn't have enough money to feed them!" Then Andrew, Simon Peter's brother, spoke up.

DESIGNED TO CREATE

"There's a young boy here with five barley loaves and two fish. But what good is that with this huge crowd?" "Tell everyone to sit down," Jesus said. So they all sat down on the grassy slopes. (The men alone numbered about 5,000.) Then Jesus took the loaves, gave thanks to God, and distributed them to the people. Afterward he did the same with the fish. And they all ate as much as they wanted. After everyone was full, Jesus told his disciples, "Now gather the leftovers, so that nothing is wasted." So they picked up the pieces and filled twelve baskets with scraps left by the people who had eaten from the five barley loaves. When the people saw him do this miraculous sign, they exclaimed, "Surely, he is the Prophet we have been expecting!"
John 6:1-14, NLT

First of all, how cool is it that God multiplied this food and fed 5000 people? This is amazing! We've heard this story of the boy with the loaves and the fish, but we forget that he was ordinary and also obedient. Clearly, someone had to ask him if he was willing to give up his lunch. There are three main points I want us to remember from this:

1. God wants you to show up. He wants to do it with you. There is power in showing up for what God has for you. He created you here on purpose, with a purpose, set apart for this world. God knew this boy would be there with his lunch and that Jesus would multiply it. When we show up in our everyday moments, do we ask God what He wants to create through us, or do we just show up to receive?

We must show up focused on the goal and the race we are running. During the *Rescue Run*, I had to show up for the victims first. They couldn't show up for themselves; somebody had to do it, and for some reason, God picked me. Beforehand, I had to be focused on training and nourishment (like 5000 calories a day), and during the

INTENTIONALLY DESIGNED

race, I had to remember why I was running in the first place, which is for the victims who didn't have the choice to quit. I had to show up and run with focus because if I didn't train well, I could injure my body. We're called to show up—boldly, intentionally, and fully present. We show up to fight for justice. We show up to love our neighbors like Jesus would. We show up to lead and serve in our homes with grace. We show up in prayer, in worship, and in the quiet moments with God. Because when we show up filled with His presence, **we show up as light in a world that desperately needs it.**

2. It takes sacrifice. Sacrifice costs us something. This ordinary boy gave up his meal. That was probably all the food he had for the day, and I wonder if he questioned whether he would go hungry that day.

When I did the rescue run, I had to sacrifice my time, energy, and resources to what God's plan was and what He wanted me to do. You guys, I didn't have time for social media or to just hang out with my friends unless they wanted to go on an eighteen-mile run with me. For every ten miles I ran, I had to sit in an ice bath. I cold plunged before cold plunging was cool. I had to visit a clinic and have a blister popped under my toenail so I could keep running. I sacrificed my dang toenails, ladies. I had to sacrifice my available hours to save money for school. It seems like such a simple thing, but there is always a cost. Last I checked, God gave the greatest sacrifice—His son, Jesus.

3. God can take the ordinary and do the extraordinary.

Jesus took the loaves and fish and multiplied them beyond anything the boy could do on his own . . . there were leftovers! Apart from God, we can't do anything, but with God, all things are possible. This boy gave his best, and God did the rest.

DESIGNED TO CREATE

Sometimes, we forget that we have the ingredients in our hands, and even though we don't have the end result, we must remember God is the miracle worker.

You guys, I simply said yes to God. I was obedient, and God showed up. BECAUSE GOD ALWAYS DOES. My ordinary passion for running and combating human trafficking went beyond anything I could do on my own.

Here are some of the things that came out of it. This is the reaping of the harvest:

- Two news coverages and a newspaper article brought awareness on a much larger scale than we could ourselves.
- Raised $20,000 to go towards a safe house, which is currently up and running.
- Met a lady who had come out of trafficking seven years prior to my rescue run. She was inspired, ran to Jesus, and started a non-profit to fight this injustice by educating and raising awareness about this topic.
- The Washington County Advocates for Human Trafficking was started.
- People want to find out how they can use their gifts, talents, and resources to continue to raise awareness about this injustice.

God took what was ordinary and made it extraordinary. God wants to creatively do the extraordinary now in and through you and me. Maybe you feel like God is asking you to do or give something beyond what you can handle. Maybe you love the idea but have no idea where to start. Maybe you don't feel equipped, good enough, or influential enough. Maybe you feel like you are living in the darkness, but LIGHT always overcomes the darkness.

We get to do it with God. We aren't alone. We don't have to figure it all out. He will direct our steps. It is in our

INTENTIONALLY DESIGNED

weakness that God is strong. Where we humble ourselves and say, "God, this is way beyond me."

> "But He said to me, 'My grace is sufficient for you, for my power is made perfect in weakness.' Therefore I will boast all the more gladly about my weaknesses, so that Christ's power may rest on me. That is why, for Christ's sake, I delight in weaknesses, in insults, in hardships, in persecutions, in difficulties. For when I am weak, then I am strong."
> 2 Corinthians 12:9-10

We have been gifted with talents and abilities and designed for a purpose. Recognizing these gifts and discerning how they align with God's will is the first step toward co-creation. It requires a heart attuned to His voice and a willingness to step out in faith. Ephesians 2:10 reminds us that "we are God's handiwork, created in Christ Jesus to do good works, which God prepared in advance for us to do." This verse highlights that our creative endeavors are part of a divine plan. We fulfill our design as co-creators by seeking God's direction and dedicating our gifts to His service.

Co-creation with God is a daily practice that involves intentionality and discipline. It might mean setting aside time for prayer and reflection, where we seek His guidance for our projects. It could include collaborating with others and recognizing that God often works through community.

Practical steps:
1. Daily Prayer and Reflection: Meet with God and ask questions.
2. Developing Your Gifts: Hone your skills and talents as an act of worship.
3. Collaborating with Others: Partner with fellow believers to bring God's vision to fruition.
4. Listening and Obeying: Be attentive to the Holy

DESIGNED TO CREATE

Spirit and willing to act on His promptings.

Co-creation is not without its challenges. We may face doubts, fear of failure, or external obstacles. However, the rewards far outweigh the difficulties. There is a deep sense of fulfillment and joy that comes from knowing we are part of God's creative work.

When we overcome challenges through faith and perseverance, we grow in our relationship with God and understanding of our purpose. The process itself becomes a testament to God's faithfulness and our trust in His plans. It starts with faith, and we walk by faith, not by sight, amen?

Hearing from those who have embraced the call to co-create can be incredibly inspiring. Consider the story of a woman who felt led to start a community garden, providing fresh produce to her neighborhood while fostering fellowship and outreach. Or the testimony of an artist who uses her talents to create worship experiences that draw others closer to God.

These stories remind us that co-creation takes many forms and that each act of creativity, no matter how small, can have a significant impact.

Lord,

Thank You for inviting us to be co-creators with You. Help us discern Your will and use our gifts for Your glory. Fill us with Your Spirit, that we may create in partnership with You, bringing Your light and love to the world.

Let Heaven come.
Amen.

INTENTIONALLY DESIGNED

Chapter 9:
Designed to Rest

In a world that praises hustle and glorifies being busy, rest often feels like a weakness—or worse, a waste of time. But what if rest isn't laziness? What if it's holy? What if God designed rest not just as a break from life, but as a way to live fully in Him?

Rest is established at the very beginning of the Bible. Genesis 2:2-3 says, "And on the seventh day God finished his work that he had done, and he rested on the seventh day from all his work that he had done. So God blessed the seventh day and made it holy, because on it God rested from all his work that he had done in creation."

We read that after six days of creation, God rested on the seventh day. This intentional act of resting was not because God was tired, but to set a pattern for us to follow. As humans, we do get tired; we aren't all-powerful. God was laying a foundation for us. The Sabbath, a day of rest, was created for humanity's benefit, reminding us that we are not merely human doings but human beings.

I used to say things like "Never miss a Monday" . . . anyone else? Monday, we grind and get 'er done. I used to view Mondays as a day to catch up on all the things I felt obligated to get done. To preface, I'm a stay-at-home mom to three kids and our golden retriever, Goose, so my traditional work week isn't quite the same as people who have to log in or go to work. I started using my Mondays as a rest day because, truthfully, for me, Monday is the start of my week, not Sunday. I was inspired to do this by joining the Revelation Wellness Love Paced Race, and they

INTENTIONALLY DESIGNED

always had Monday as a rest day. I recently read *Tired of Being Tired* by Jess Connolly, which talks about how it was always night and then day in Genesis. So rest comes before work. This is a simple way I've rearranged and structured my week to change my mindset on Mondays, from madness to a place of rest.

When I treated Monday as a rest day, my Mondays weren't so horrible. It was still an adjustment as my husband would go back to work, but I chose to be a little more laid back as a mom on those days as well. It's one of my favorite days of the week now. Since Monday is now, for me, seen as the first day of the week, I wanted to start my week intentionally with rest.

True rest is not just about physical relaxation but encompasses mental, emotional, and spiritual rejuvenation. It also allows us to enjoy what God created and simply be. We don't just live to work. We rest with God, and everything flows out of that relationship. Jesus extends an invitation to all who are weary and burdened to come to Him for rest (Matthew 11:28-30). This rest is found in our relationship with Him, where we can lay down our burdens and find peace for our souls. Sadly, I find most people who are tired and exhausted are not going to Jesus for rest at all. We look for the next best thing over and over again, and nothing seems to satisfy us. Jesus didn't die for us to be buffet-style Christians, picking and choosing what seems nice. What if we went to God first, even in our rest?

I don't know about you, but the world has felt very weary and heavy at times. It's left me exhausted over and over again. Many of us don't prioritize rest.

Things That Block Us From Rest:

- Trying to Stay Relevant
- Doom Scrolling

DESIGNED TO REST

- The News
- Chasing Money or Position
- Overpacked Schedule
- The Need to Be Productive
- Fear of Missing Out

We must recognize these obstacles and address them head-on. If we know what the obstacles are, we can get to the root issue, rather than putting a band-aid on it. Setting boundaries, learning to say no, and trusting God with our time can help us create space for rest. Rest is essential for our health and well-being. It allows our bodies to heal, our minds to refresh, and our spirits to be renewed. Without adequate rest, we become susceptible to stress, anxiety, and burnout. Rest helps us be more productive, creative, and effective in our work and ministries. Have you ever felt stuck on something and stepped away for fifteen minutes, only to come back and find it helped? Resting rejuvenates us and allows us to keep on going.

God designed us to both cultivate and rest. They aren't in competition—they're in partnership. But if we're honest, we often treat them like enemies. Like, if we're resting, we must not be doing enough. And if we're working hard, there's no time to slow down.

We grind in the name of faithfulness. We hustle in the name of obedience. But here's the truth: **Rest isn't weakness. It's warfare.** Rest is where we let God do the heart-work while we step out of the hustle. It's not the opposite of cultivation—it's what makes true cultivation sustainable. Rest sustains the work God calls us to. Maybe the reason you feel like you're running on empty is because you've been pouring from a place God never asked you to pour from.

Rest is for RESTORATION. And I love to think of that word *restore* like this: **RE-STORY.**

INTENTIONALLY DESIGNED

God is rewriting what you believe about productivity, about purpose, and about your pace. You weren't made to live burned out for the Kingdom. You were made to co-labor with God—planting seeds *and* letting Him water them while you sleep. So no, rest and cultivation aren't at war. But the enemy would love for you to think they are—because as long as you keep choosing hustle over healing, he knows you'll eventually wear out.

I'm the queen of making up stories in my head about people's hidden agendas, how they actually think about me, or how they'll respond to a text or something I say. I was taking those thoughts captive and resubmitting them to the Lord, but they kept coming back. After years of this struggle, I decided if I had the ability when this happened, I should eat a snack and take a nap. **God was helping me RE-STORY my mind** from overanalyzing. He put my mind at rest by taking a nap. Sometimes rest is practical—like a nap or a walk. And sometimes, it's spiritual—like releasing the need to carry what only God can.

> *"The Lord is my shepherd; I shall not want. He makes me lie down in green pastures. He leads me beside still waters. He restores my soul."*
> *Psalm 23:1-3*

How many of us feel like our minds won't turn off, yet we won't try to do the very thing that would help us? Rest. We are quick to grab a coffee or energy drink to keep going, and in doing so, we're making ourselves more tired. Research says that for every night of inadequate sleep, it takes one week to help your brain come back to normal. Well, I've had three kids, and let me tell you, I can't wait for my brain to be back. So, let's get practical.

If soul rest feels abstract, here are some small, practical ways to welcome God into your rhythms.

1. Keep the Sabbath: Set aside a specific day each

week to rest and focus on God. Use this as a day for worship in all that you do. Pick activities for yourself and your family that are rejuvenating.

2. **Daily Rhythms:** Incorporate moments of rest into your daily routine. This could be having slow mornings, specific prayer times, meditation, walking in nature, or simply pausing to breathe deeply. It's adding in practical, attainable rhythms.

3. **Digital Detox:** Take regular breaks from technology to disconnect from the noise and reconnect with yourself and God. Have a specific time of day that you turn it off or set a screen time limit.

4. **Restorative Activities:** Engage in activities that bring you joy and relaxation. Here are a few examples: reading, gardening, walking, or spending time with loved ones.

5. **Meditate on God's Word:** Meditation can help your mind focus on the present moment, reminding you of the truth and who God is.

Sample Rest Day Schedule: Here's an example of what a rest day might look like—focused on both soul and body:

- **8:00 AM** – Wake up without an alarm, make coffee or tea
- **8:30 AM** – Read Scripture, journal, or simply sit in silence
- **9:30 AM** – Go for a walk in nature or light stretching
- **11:00 AM** – Connect with a friend or family member without distraction
- **12:00 PM** – Prepare a slow meal and eat mindfully
- **1:00 PM** – Nap or lie down with no agenda
- **3:00 PM** – Read a life-giving book or do a creative

INTENTIONALLY DESIGNED

hobby
- **5:00 PM** – Listen to worship music or soak in Scripture
- **6:00 PM** – Cook and eat a simple dinner
- **7:30 PM** – Reflect on the day and what God showed you
- **9:00 PM** – Light a candle, put screens away, prepare for rest

Rest is not just a break from work but an act of worship. I once was in worship, and somebody fell asleep during the set. It could be easy to take offense, but I remembered that they were in the presence of God. They were resting in the presence of the Lord, and that too is worship. How often do we tell people not to rest with God but to get up and "look alive." By resting, we acknowledge our dependence on God and trust in His provision. It is a declaration that our worth is not based on our productivity but on our identity as children of God. We trust that our Father will take care of us because He also cares for the sparrows. In rest, we find the strength to fulfill our purpose and the grace to co-create with Him.

We were designed to rest. It is a gift from God, a vital part of our design, and essential for our holistic well-being. Embracing rest allows us to live fully and abundantly, as God intended. It's how we learn to LIVE WITH GOD, not just live for God. As we learn to rest in Him, we discover a deeper sense of peace, purpose, and joy in our lives. Rest is not just a quick fix but a lifestyle. It is an ongoing journey of learning to balance work and rest, productivity and stillness, and doing and being. I pray we continually seek God's guidance and grace to live a life intentionally designed for rest.

Doesn't it make sense that the enemy would want us worked down to the bone and exhausted? That he'd want us to try and achieve our worth and love from our Heavenly Father? God's love is free for the taking. The

DESIGNED TO REST

gospel is what God did, not what we did.

> *"For God so loved the world, that he gave his only Son, that whoever believes in him should not perish but have eternal life."*
> John 3:16

The enemy wants us exhausted, so we miss out on the moments with God. The enemy wants us to believe the gospel requires us to be the ones to save others and ourselves. Thank God He sent us the Holy Spirit. It's not in our power but in HIS that people are saved. We can rest in the promise that God's got it. His kingdom is still coming, even if we need to take a snack break and a nap. We are not in control.

Rest isn't optional. It's essential. It's how we live *with* God, not just *for* Him.

I think of the story of Jesus asleep on the boat in the midst of a storm. The majority of us focus on storms in our lives, but Jesus was at peace. How could He be at peace in a moment like that? How could He rest during that? Was He not thinking about the storm at all? Was He just a deep sleeper?

Just as Jesus found rest amidst the storm, you can too. You can still find rest in the chaotic moments of your life. In the middle of a storm, He slept—not just physically, but from a place of deep soul rest. His body may have been still, but it was His spirit that was at peace. The disciples panicked, overwhelmed by fear, but Jesus trusted. He wasn't just taking a nap; He was anchored in the unshakable truth of who His Father was. His rest revealed a soul fully surrendered to the sovereignty of God, a heart untroubled by the chaos around Him because He knew who held the waves.

Rest isn't about having a perfect sleep schedule

INTENTIONALLY DESIGNED

(especially if you're a mom!). But here are some practical ways to get the rest your body and soul need:

1. Create a Consistent Sleep Schedule: Go to bed and wake up at the same time every day. This is easier said than done. I'm a mom of three little ones, so my schedule is inconsistent, but I've found that the earlier I hop into bed, the better, because some sleep is better than none.

2. Create a Restful Environment: I did interior design for a few years, and one of my favorite things to do is design a room that looks and feels restful — a space that gives me permission to cast my cares away.

3. Limit Screen Time Before Bed: My personal rule is no screens one hour before bed, unless I fall asleep watching a movie, then it doesn't count! The blue light can affect your ability to fall asleep, so try to steer clear of it.

4. Living an Active Lifestyle: Regular physical activity can promote better sleep and help you fall asleep faster.

5. Tart Cherry Juice: It's a natural source of melatonin. Melatonin is a hormone that regulates the sleep-wake cycles. It is also anti-inflammatory and full of antioxidants. Give me a tart cherry mocktail, and I'll probably fall asleep mid-conversation within thirty minutes.

6. Magnesium Lotion: Magnesium helps us relax our muscles, which can help relieve tension in our bodies. Magnesium can also help calm our nervous system. Using it in a lotion form helps it absorb through the skin. Apply a small amount to your legs or the bottoms of your feet.

DESIGNED TO REST

7. Comfy Pajamas: Pajamas can either make or break a night of sleep, so pick some you feel the best in.

Bonus Soul-Care Practice: Brain Dump. If your mind feels cluttered or chaotic, try doing a brain dump. Grab a notebook or journal and write down everything swirling in your head—your to-do lists, worries, thoughts, reminders, or even prayers. It doesn't need to be pretty or organized. Just get it all out. When we release the mental clutter onto paper, we create space in our minds and hearts for peace. A brain dump helps shift our focus from internal overwhelm to external surrender. It can be a first step toward clarity, calm, and soul rest.

By incorporating simple practices like these, we can better prepare ourselves to receive the rest God has for us. **God's plan for rest is to restore your soul.**

You weren't created to carry it all. You weren't just designed to work hard—you were designed to walk with God. Rest is not just permission—it's an invitation. To let go. To breathe deep. To trust again. He's not looking for your hustle; He's inviting you to His heart. God gave you this gift. You don't have to earn it. Just receive it.

Gracious Lord,

Thank You for designing me not only for work but also for rest. In a world that glorifies busyness, remind me that true rest is found in You. Teach me to embrace stillness and to trust that You are working even when I am not. Help me to find peace in Your presence, knowing that You sustain me. May I rest in Your love, and may my soul be refreshed as I honor the rhythms of grace You have set for my life.

In Jesus' name,
Amen.

INTENTIONALLY DESIGNED

Chapter 10: Designed to Worship

We are always in a state of worship—what changes is who or what we are worshiping. Let that sink in. Worship is a profound act of honor and reverence. It is an expression of connection. Worship is a way of life, not thirty minutes on a Sunday. Worship is the overflow of our lives to God's glory. When I think about worship, I am reminded of the story of King David dancing before the Lord with all his might, unashamed and fully immersed in his love for God.

> *"And David danced before the Lord with all his might. And David was wearing a linen ephod."*
> 2 Samuel 6:14

This image captures the essence of worship – a heartfelt, uninhibited expression of adoration and reverence for our Creator. We were created to worship. Worship is often associated with singing songs, hymns, or attending church services, but its true essence goes far beyond these activities. Worship is an attitude of the heart, a lifestyle that permeates every aspect of our lives. Jesus tells us that true worshipers will worship the Father in spirit and truth. This means that worship is not confined to a specific place or time but is a continuous, sincere expression of our love for God.

> *"But the hour is coming, and is now here, when the true worshipers will worship the Father in spirit and truth, for the Father is seeking such people to worship him. God is spirit, and those who worship him must worship in spirit and truth."*
> John 4:23-24

INTENTIONALLY DESIGNED

If we aren't careful to worship the Lord in spirit and truth, we can end up worshiping idols. An idol isn't just a golden calf; it's anything we turn to in place of God or chase after to fulfill us. For example, many people today idolize success, constantly striving for career achievements, recognition, or material wealth. The pursuit of these things can easily replace our focus on God, especially when we begin to place our identity and worth in them rather than in Him. Just like the Israelites became impatient and turned to a physical idol, we, too, can turn to something else when we feel restless or discontent. So my question is this: what is your life leading you toward? Is it leading you to Jesus or to something else that can never truly satisfy?

"Whatever you do, work heartily, as for the Lord and not for men, knowing that from the Lord you will receive the inheritance as your reward. You are serving the Lord Christ."
Colossians 3:23-24

Worship is doing everything we do unto the Lord, not for the approval of man. As a worship leader, I want to set the record straight: we are all worship leaders. It's not just the people who stand on stage, microphone in hand, looking cool and hipster. Whether you can sing like a professional or are tone deaf, whether you can strum a guitar or struggle to keep a beat, you are a worship leader. Worship is about how we lead ourselves and others in every moment of our lives.

So, how are you leading? Are you pointing people toward God, encouraging them to lay down their idols and glorify Him? Or are you leading them toward something else? Worship is not just about music or performances; it's about hearts being aligned with God's heart. I often hear people say worship leaders are responsible for "leading the congregation into a response," but I believe worship starts with our own hearts. **You can only lead others as far as you've gone yourself.** You can't give away what

DESIGNED TO WORSHIP

you don't have. As a worship leader, my primary role is to fix my eyes on Jesus. Every moment of worship, whether in song or action, should flow out of my love for Him.

Imagine if every worship service were filled with people whose hearts were genuinely fixed on Jesus—where we were all focused on the Lord, not distracted by ourselves or our surroundings. Those are the moments of worship that carry the deepest significance. My job as a worship leader isn't just to hype people up or make them feel good. It's to keep my eyes on Heaven, to lead by example. We aren't serving man through worship; we are serving God, glorifying Him in spirit and truth.

If we focus too much on our gifts and talents in worship, we miss the point. What happens when those things are taken away—when we can't sing, lead, or play like we did before? I always say, "Give God your best, and let Him do the rest." Worship is living with excellence, but it also means being flexible—being ready to change direction as God leads us, whether in a worship service or in the moments of our daily lives.

How can we lead in worship, both positively and negatively? Leading positively means focusing on Jesus—pointing ourselves and others toward Him, leading with humility, authenticity, and a heart of service. It's about helping others encounter the living God. On the other hand, we can lead negatively when we focus on ourselves: our performance, our image, or what people think of us. When we're distracted by pride or the need for approval, we're no longer leading others toward God. Instead, we're pulling them away from the very focus of worship.

Worship is not about getting God's attention because He is already looking at you. Worship is about locking eyes with God, remembering who He is, and responding to His love. It's a continual act of realigning our hearts with His. That's the heart of worship and how we lead others in it.

INTENTIONALLY DESIGNED

Forms of Worship:
- Corporate Worship
- Personal Worship

Corporate worship is when we gather in agreement to honor and glorify God. It is where more than one person is gathering. Personal worship is an integral part of our everyday lives, where we give God honor and glory. Here are some examples: Prayer, singing, journaling, meditating, running, resting, changing diapers, and so much more.

"I appeal to you therefore, brothers, by the mercies of God, to present your bodies as a living sacrifice, holy and acceptable to God, which is your spiritual worship."
Romans 12:1

Worship is not just a Sunday morning activity but a way of life. It involves dedicating our thoughts, actions, and attitudes to God daily. This means being mindful of His presence in our daily routines and seeking to honor Him in everything we do. There are many ways to incorporate worship into our daily lives. We can start our day with prayer, thanking God for His blessings and seeking His guidance. Throughout the day, we can practice gratitude, recognizing God's hand in the big and small moments. Acts of service, whether helping a neighbor or volunteering at a local charity, are also forms of worship, as they reflect God's love and compassion for the world around us.

How can we worship God if we don't know who He is? Many people are no longer opening their Bibles and are being spoon-fed the word of God, and thinking it'll transform their lives. One way we worship God is by actually knowing Him. When we know God, we know who we are. One thing that glorifies God is when we walk in the identity of being His child.

True worship comes from a sincere heart. Isaiah

DESIGNED TO WORSHIP

29:13 warns against worshiping with lips while our hearts are far from God. Jesus echoes this sentiment in Matthew 15:8-9, emphasizing that worship must be genuine and not just an outward show: *"'This people honors me with their lips, but their heart is far from me; in vain do they worship me, teaching as doctrines the commandments of men."*

Pride comes before the fall. Lucifer fell because He wanted to be worshiped.

At the core of worship is our personal relationship with God. Worship draws us closer to Him, allowing us to experience His presence and love more deeply. It is through worship that we express our love for God and acknowledge His greatness and sovereignty. When we prioritize having a heart of worship, it strengthens our relationship with God. When we ask ourselves the question: Would this action glorify God? Why would it? Or why wouldn't it? We give way to remembering what the Bible says, the truth, and the importance of living by the Spirit. When we continuously worship God, our relationship with him grows stronger.

"Now the Lord is the Spirit, and where the Spirit of the Lord is, there is freedom."
2 Corinthians 3:17

More often than not, I see people struggle in worship times. A lot of people have associated worship with "feeling" like God is near, when the truth of the matter is that He is with you all the time. Some people also say they struggle with the "style of worship." **Worship isn't a genre. Worship is your heart posture.** I love this analogy, so bear with me for a moment. Imagine holding a cup of coffee and someone runs into you. What goes flying out of the coffee cup? Coffee, right? Why not matcha or chai? Why? Because what you pour into the cup is what comes out. If you fill it with coffee, coffee will spill out. If you fill

INTENTIONALLY DESIGNED

the cup with matcha, matcha will come out. If you fill the cup with chai, chai will come out. What are you filling your heart with? This isn't about whether the cup is half full or empty. In God's kingdom, it's overflowing. Is your heart focused on Jesus and the truth so that it's overflowing with Him? Does God have your whole heart?

I like to examine our hearts like they are a well. If you don't stir up the water in the well, the well will get stagnant. Have you ever looked at stagnant water? It is not something I want entering my body. So, how can you fan the flame or stir up the well of your heart? In our busy lives, it can be challenging to maintain a heart of worship. Distractions, busyness, and spiritual dryness are common barriers that can hinder our worship. However, when we confront these challenges head-on, we can take steps to overcome them.

One way to overcome distractions is to set aside specific times for worship and stick to them. Creating a dedicated space for prayer and worship can also help minimize distractions. When we feel spiritually dry, it is important to remember that worship is not about our feelings but about honoring God. During these times, we can seek encouragement from fellow believers, immerse ourselves in God's Word, and continue to worship even when it feels difficult.

I swapped out screen time for my kids with worship, whether it be worship music in the car, pulling out the guitar, hitting play on Spotify, or casting worship music on YouTube. It changed my heart during the day. I saw evidence of the spirit in my life because I was experiencing fruit.

While personal worship is essential, corporate worship—worshiping together as a community of believers —is equally important. Gathering with others to praise and glorify God strengthens our faith and fosters a sense of unity and belonging. In corporate worship,

DESIGNED TO WORSHIP

we experience the beauty of diversity within the body of Christ. People from different backgrounds, cultures, and walks of life come together, united by their love for God. This unity in diversity reflects the Kingdom of God and reminds us that we are part of something much greater than ourselves.

Worship is warfare. When God led people into battle throughout Scripture, He sent the worshippers first. Worship isn't just adoration and reverence toward God. It's knowing who He is, which is a powerful weapon. Worship is a strategic move in the battle against the enemy. When we worship, we are fixing our eyes on the truth, which shines light on the lies we may be believing.

In the Bible, there was a man named Jehoshaphat, who was the king of Judah. Jehoshaphat saw a threat, turned to God in prayer, and had people fast throughout the land. God promised victory, but His strategy wasn't sending the strongest warriors to the front lines. Jehoshaphat anointed singers to go ahead of the army. They were to praise and proclaim the beauty and holiness of God.

> *"And when he had taken counsel with the people, he appointed those who were to sing to the Lord and praise him in holy attire, as they went before the army, and say, 'Give thanks to the Lord, for his steadfast love endures forever.' And when they began to sing and praise, the Lord set an ambush against the men of Ammon, Moab, and Mount Seir, who had come against Judah, so that they were routed. For the men of Ammon and Moab rose against the inhabitants of Mount Seir, devoting them to destruction, and when they had made an end of the inhabitants of Seir, they all helped to destroy one another.*
> 2 Chronicles 20:21-23

This account demonstrates the power of worship to

INTENTIONALLY DESIGNED

change the spiritual atmosphere and bring about divine intervention. Worship shifts our focus from the problem to the Problem Solver, from the battle to the Victor.

Worship is not just a response to God's goodness but a declaration of His sovereignty over every situation. When we worship, we align ourselves with God's perspective, acknowledging His power and authority. This act of faith can dismantle the enemy's plans and bring God's purposes to fruition.

Paul and Silas experienced the power of worship in Acts 16. After being beaten and thrown into prison, they prayed and sang hymns to God. Their worship led to a miraculous earthquake that opened the prison doors and loosened their chains. Not only were they set free, but their act of worship also led to the salvation of the jailer and his entire household.

In our lives, we may face battles that seem insurmountable. Whether it is a health crisis, financial difficulties, or relational struggles, we can turn to worship as our weapon. When we lift our voices in praise, we invite God's presence into our circumstances, and His presence changes everything.

Worship is an act of trust, declaring that God is bigger than our battles and His plans will prevail. It is a reminder that our fight is not against flesh and blood but against spiritual forces (Ephesians 6:12). By worshiping, we put on the armor of God, standing firm in His strength and victory.

Practical Ways to Worship:

1. Praise and Thanksgiving: Start by thanking God for His goodness and faithfulness. Reflect on His past victories in your life and express your gratitude.
2. Singing: Lift your voice in song, whether through

hymns, contemporary worship songs, or spontaneous praise. Music has a unique ability to connect our hearts with God.
3. Scripture: Meditate on and declare God's promises found in the Bible. Use His Word as a foundation for your worship and a reminder of His truth.
4. Prayer: Engage in prayerful worship, expressing your love and adoration for God. Let your prayers be filled with praise and acknowledgment of His greatness.
5. Lifestyle: Worship is not limited to specific moments but is a way of life. Live in a manner that honors God, making choices that reflect your devotion to Him.

As we have seen, we are designed to worship. Worship is not just a part of our Christian life; it is central to our identity as followers of Christ. By living a lifestyle of worship, both individually and in community, we draw closer to God and fulfill our purpose as His creation. Let us embrace our design to worship and seek to honor God in every aspect of our lives.

Ways to Reflect on Worship:

- Reflect on your daily routines and identify ways to incorporate worship into your everyday life.
- Make a conscious effort to worship with sincerity and authenticity, focusing on your personal relationship with God.
- Participate in corporate worship and seek to build unity within your community of believers.
- When faced with barriers to worship, remember the importance of honoring God and take practical steps to overcome those challenges.

INTENTIONALLY DESIGNED

Heavenly Father,

Thank You for creating us with purpose and intention, designed to worship You in all we do. We come before You today with hearts full of gratitude for Your love, Your grace, and the opportunity to know You more. May we always remember that worship isn't just found in songs or rituals, but in the daily act of living in alignment with Your truth.

Lord, help us lay down anything that hinders our worship—whether it be distractions, fears, or the lies of the world. Teach us to fix our eyes on You, to honor You with every breath, decision, and moment. May our lives reflect Your glory and Your goodness, and may we worship You in spirit and in truth.

We ask that You continue to reveal Yourself to us in deeper ways, so that our worship grows ever richer and more genuine. Fill us with Your Holy Spirit and empower us to live as true worshippers—living lives that bring You praise and make Your name known.

Thank You for making us *designed to worship*. We are Yours, and we give You all the glory and honor, now and forever.

In Jesus' name,
Amen.

PART THREE: LIVING BOLDLY IN FREEDOM

INTENTIONALLY DESIGNED

Chapter 11: Designed for Such a Time as This

You were designed to be a part of God's story. Your life is to give Him glory. You were designed for this day and time. Sadly, more often than not, I hear people say they were born in the wrong generation, but God created and crafted you for the here and now. If we don't pay attention to what God is doing and saying, we may just miss out on what He has for us. You've probably heard the phrase "for such a time as this" before, but if you haven't, it is from the book of Esther in the Bible. This is a beautiful story of courage, faith, and God's divine timing. Our world is very unpredictable at times and often chaotic. When we understand that God designed us for the time we are alive, it is empowering to step into our God-given roles with confidence and purpose.

God's timing is right where I want to be. Have you ever been in the wrong place at the wrong time? Maybe you walked into a conversation with somebody talking about you behind your back? Was it truly the wrong place at the wrong time, or was God trying to show you that maybe that friend wasn't as trustworthy as you thought? I think it's time we switch the narrative and stop saying things like we are in the wrong place at the wrong time, and instead ask God where He is in the room. I think we often focus on the event we're attending instead of what God is doing. What is His plan? How does He want us to participate?

Esther's bravery and willingness to act at the right time ultimately led to the salvation of her people. Her story is a testament to the importance of noticing and embracing the moments we are uniquely positioned for. Just as Esther was positioned for a specific time

INTENTIONALLY DESIGNED

and purpose, we, too, are placed in our unique contexts for reasons possibly beyond our understanding. God strategically places us to help fulfill His purposes.

Esther was an orphaned Jewish girl who became queen of Persia. Her story, detailed in the Book of Esther, unfolds in a time of great peril for the Jewish people. Haman, a high-ranking official, devised a plot to annihilate all Jews in the kingdom. Unaware of Esther's Jewish heritage, Haman's decree placed her in a precarious position. When Esther's cousin, Mordecai, learned of the plot, he urged her to use her influence with the king to save their people. Initially hesitant, Esther feared for her life, knowing that approaching the king unsummoned could result in death. However, Mordecai's words resonated deeply:

> "And who knows but that you have come to your royal position for such a time as this?"
> Esther 4:14

Esther could have died when she went into the presence of Haman, but she went forward with bravery to save the Jewish people. She used her voice instead of just letting people be killed. But most people don't realize that what Mordecai said to Esther wasn't about favor; it was a rebuke.

"You have come to your royal position for such a time as this?"

Basically, he is saying, Esther, wake up! It's time to lay down your royalty for the sake of others. He's telling her to set aside her agenda, her ambitions, her interests, and her pride and face the enemy head-on. So, what does that look like in our own lives? What labels and titles are we holding onto that are holding us hostage? Where do we feel silenced? His rebuke as a family member changed the game for the Jewish people. It saved so many lives.

DESIGNED FOR SUCH A TIME AS THIS

There was no promise of a positive outcome. Esther simply stood up for what was right and was willing to be a living sacrifice for her people. Our responsibility is obedience; God's role is the outcome. As we discussed earlier, we are planting seeds, and it's God that makes them grow.

> *"I appeal to you therefore, brothers, by the mercies of God, to present your bodies as a living sacrifice, holy and acceptable to God, which is your spiritual worship. Do not be conformed to this world, but be transformed by the renewal of your mind, that by testing you may discern what is the will of God, what is good and acceptable and perfect."*
> Romans 12:1-2

The first step we need to take is to turn around and look at Jesus face-to-face. Some of us have been trying to build our own kingdom instead of God's. In the world, we build our own kingdoms, but in God's kingdom, we help build His. It starts with repentance. We need to apologize and ask for forgiveness. We don't always want to run to the altar and sacrifice. The second thing we need to do is understand that our identity is only in the fact that we are a child of God. Any job or title can be ripped away from us. When we stand on the foundation and know our identity, we respond out of that place and start to understand our role in the Kingdom of God.

A few years ago, I was obsessed with interior design. I worked really hard to build a business, and I had my own Instagram for it—Hannmade For The Home. In some people's eyes, I was probably looked at as successful. I built over 1k followers, which is honestly a really hard thing to do with no prior knowledge of SEO or hashtags. I provided interior design consultations to individuals. I posted links to try to make any money I could to help my family, since we lived off one income. I had clients here and there, but it didn't take off like I thought it would. I took many courses on growing an Instagram business, and nothing seemed to

INTENTIONALLY DESIGNED

work. When I felt God ask me to write this book, I felt Him ask me to give Him Hannmade For The Home fully. I needed to give up being known as an interior designer. I needed to give up the responsibility of having to bring income into our family and trust that, as my Heavenly Father, He would provide it. I was building my own kingdom. Now, I'm not saying that if you have a successful business, you are building your own kingdom, but God knew my heart. I was putting in the work, and I honestly believe God didn't let it grow because He knew I was made for something completely different. I do believe God gave me the gift, but I wasn't using it for the right purposes. I was putting trust into my own hands, and honestly, I was really struggling in my relationship with God. God let that title be taken away from me. I remember the day I took my website down, and the world kept going. The world didn't even notice, honestly. Do I still love interior design? Absolutely. But, I felt like I was more focused on things that don't go to Heaven versus being focused on Heaven coming down to Earth.

I hear women say this phrase all the time, *"I'm just waiting on God."* **But waiting on God isn't passive. While we wait on God, we do the next best thing.** While we wait on God, we believe He will do it, and we show up like we are a part of the solution. If Esther had been passive, she would most likely have ended up dead along with all the other Jewish people. Many of us are waiting for another confirmation when God already told us what to do. A lot of us keep delaying our obedience because of fear. We're afraid of letting God down, what others will think, and what we have to give up, afraid of failing, and so many more. If God told you to step back and be passive, then be obedient, but if you're waiting on God and nothing is happening, you might need to do the next best thing. **Are you willing to be the answer to the prayer you are praying?**

When God first told me to write this book, I was on a trip to Dallas with some ladies from my church. I had never written a book or had a desire to do so. I spent an entire

DESIGNED FOR SUCH A TIME AS THIS

year talking about writing a book, but I wasn't spending time researching how to do it, who it was for, or what it would be about. I spent a year in straight disobedience because I lived in apathy and was waiting on God to have it all fall into my lap. I took a course through Go & Tell Gals called Go Teams, and I quickly realized how much time I had wasted. Now, as I'm writing to you, I do brain-dumps on the weekly of thoughts and ask God how I can serve women who want to go deeper in their relationship with God.

Believing we are designed for specific moments starts with recognizing God's sovereignty. What is God's sovereignty? God's sovereignty is understanding that God is king, He's in control, He has the best plan, and He is present with His people. It's understanding that nothing happens outside of God's will. God's sovereignty sees the bigger picture and knows the impact of our presence and actions in the world. Trusting Him and His plan helps us find meaning in our circumstances and everyday moments.

God has given us jobs, gifts, positions, education, resources, and so much more to glorify Him and shape His kingdom. God didn't create us to do nothing. He created us to fight the good fight. We've read how God created man to cultivate the garden. It's time we get up and show up for what we were designed for.

Embrace your unique role. Each of us has a distinct combination of gifts, experiences, and opportunities that equip us for our roles, which compile our worldviews. Embracing who we are and where we are placed enables us to serve effectively. Like Esther, our backgrounds and positions can be used powerfully in God's hands. Instead of seeing our differences as divisive, we can celebrate the diversity among us and learn so much more about God simply by being around people and hearing their stories.

We live by faith, not by sight. When we live by faith, it doesn't mean we don't have fear; it means that we pick

INTENTIONALLY DESIGNED

up courage. Being designed for a time such as this often requires courage and faith. Stepping into our roles might involve risks, just as it did for Esther. However, trusting God and taking bold steps can lead to extraordinary outcomes when we are obedient to the ordinary. But first, we have to take a step of action. Maybe you don't know why you were designed for such a time as this. **You are a world changer, a chain breaker, and a kingdom builder.** We don't always believe these things about ourselves, but as we align ourselves with God and His heart, we will see them ring true.

    I grew up watching Veggie Tales. Shadrach, Meshach, and Abednego refused to bow down and worship the idol that Nebuchadnezzar wanted them to worship when the music started playing. If any of you watched Veggie Tales, you'd know it was a giant bunny. If you know, you know, and probably have it stuck in your head. Sorry, not sorry. Rack, Shach, and Benny refused to bow to a fake God. King Neb had made a law that everyone must bow to this idol or be thrown into a fiery furnace. Shach, Rack, and Benny said they would only bow down to their God and that God would deliver them. Even if He doesn't deliver them, they still wouldn't bow down to His idol made of gold. King Neb had them thrown into the fiery furnace, which was heated seven times as much as usual. King Nebuchadnezzar went to look and saw that there were four men unbound in the fire and that the fourth man looked like the Son of God. He asked the guards, "Didn't we put three men in there? It looks like there are four."

    Shadrach, Meshach, and Abednego are powerful examples of faith and courage. They were thrust into a situation where their unwavering devotion to God was tested. Refusing to bow to the king's idol, they faced the fiery furnace, believing that God would deliver them. Even if He did not, their commitment to their faith remained steadfast. Their story highlights how being faithful in the face of adversity can serve a greater purpose, showcasing that they were indeed designed for such a pivotal moment in history. And what happened after this? King Nebuchadnezzar made a decree that anyone who spoke against the God of the Jews would be torn from limb to limb and their house would be destroyed.

Shach, Rack, and Benny had an unwavering devotion to God. They knew His character and nature. They were willing to follow and honor God regardless of what the King was asking of them. A lot of us are bound in fear about sharing that we love Jesus because of others who have misrepresented God, or we are afraid of how others will view us. We're scared to put that we are Christians in our Instagram bios. Whatever it may be, the question is, are you willing to follow the Lord regardless of what the world thinks?

So maybe you still don't know what moment in time you were designed for. Here are some practical steps to take to lead you in that direction.

Practical Steps to Embrace Your Moment You Were Designed For:
Seek God's Guidance: Regularly pray and seek God's direction for your life. Ask Him to reveal the moments and opportunities He has designed for you. Stay attuned to the Holy Spirit's promptings.

Be Prepared: Just as Esther prepared through prayer and fasting, prepare yourself spiritually, emotionally, and practically. Study God's Word, develop your skills, and stay ready to act when the moment arises.

Stay Connected to Community: Surround yourself with a supportive community of believers who can encourage and guide you. Mordecai's role in Esther's life was crucial; similarly, we need people who can speak wisdom and encouragement into our lives.

Act with Purpose: When the time comes, step forward with confidence. Know that God has equipped you for

INTENTIONALLY DESIGNED

this moment. Whether it is a small act of kindness or a significant leadership decision, act with the assurance that you are part of God's greater plan.

Examples of Divine Timing in Everyday Life
In the Workplace: You might be in your job not just for career advancement but to be a light to your colleagues, bring ethical changes, or support someone in need.

In Your Community: Your involvement in local activities, through volunteering or participating in community events, can position you to make a significant impact.

In Your Family: Your role within your family, as a parent, sibling, or child, is essential. Your presence and actions can influence and inspire those closest to you.

Understanding we are designed for such a time as this fills our lives with purpose and meaning. Like Esther, we may find ourselves in situations where our actions have far-reaching consequences. By recognizing God's sovereignty, embracing our unique roles, responding with courage and faith, and acting with purpose, we can fulfill the divine appointments set before us. Every moment, every situation, is an opportunity to live out the purpose God has intricately woven into our lives. Trust in His timing and step boldly into the roles He has prepared for you. You were designed for such a time as this.

Jesus,

Search our hearts. Help us be honest: have we been building a kingdom for ourselves or for you? Lord, help us see what you have chosen and set apart for me to live. Help me focus on things above. Lord, please direct, guide, and lead me; give me the courage to step out in faith, remembering that You are who You say You are.

In Jesus' name,
Amen.

Chapter 12: Designed for the Kingdom of God

You were designed for the Kingdom of God. Plain and simple. To really understand what that means, we have to understand the world's pull versus the Kingdom's call. You see, this world is not our home. It was never meant to be. To truly live for the Kingdom of God, we must first recognize that we were created to be citizens of Heaven, even though we are living in a broken world.

In the beginning, when God created the heavens and the earth, He designed a perfect world for His creation to live in harmony with Him. This was Eden—the original kingdom of God on Earth, where Heaven and Earth intersected, and God walked among us. It was here that humanity was designed for a relationship with God, to reflect His glory and enjoy His presence forever. But sin entered, and that kingdom was fractured. The Garden of Eden was lost, and humanity was cast out. The story of the Bible is about God's work to restore that kingdom on Earth, to bring Heaven down to Earth again.

You are a citizen of Heaven. From the moment we accept Christ, we become citizens of God's Kingdom. This new identity shapes our values, priorities, and actions. You were designed for that restoration. We were made for God's Kingdom, a Kingdom that transcends what we see and feel in this world.

"But our citizenship is in heaven, and from it we await a Savior, the Lord Jesus Christ."
Philippians 3:20

You are a Kingdom Ambassador. The moment

INTENTIONALLY DESIGNED

we come to Christ, we step into a larger narrative—God's redemptive plan for the world. While we live in this broken world, we are not of it. This world isn't our home. We are ambassadors of a Kingdom yet to manifest on Earth fully. The Kingdom of God is about the restoration of what was lost in Eden, bringing Heaven to Earth, and aligning our lives with God's divine design. This understanding changes everything. It changes how we live, how we work, how we treat others, and how we view the world.

Living for the Kingdom of God means we must choose to live differently than the world around us. The world tells us to live for ourselves, build our own kingdoms, and chase after success, money, and status. But the Kingdom of God calls us to surrender our lives, to lay down our ambitions for the sake of something far greater—God's purposes. Jesus taught that when we seek first the Kingdom of God and His righteousness, everything else will follow.

"Seek the Kingdom of God above all else, and live righteously, and he will give you everything you need."
Matthew 6:33

This is not just a future hope but a present reality. The Kingdom of God is not some distant, far-off place. It's here and now, and we are called to bring it to Earth.

"Don't copy the behavior and customs of this world, but let God transform you into a new person by changing the way you think. Then you will learn to know God's will for you, which is good and pleasing and perfect."
Romans 12:2

The Kingdom of God is built on principles of love, justice, mercy, and humility. These principles stand in stark contrast to the values of the world. The world tells us to get ahead at any cost and be ruthless in our pursuit of success. Jesus shows us a different way—the way of humility, service, and sacrificial love.

DESIGNED FOR THE KINGDOM OF GOD

Jesus describes the characteristics of those who are part of His Kingdom.

> "Blessed are the poor in spirit, for theirs is the kingdom of heaven. Blessed are those who mourn, for they shall be comforted. Blessed are the meek, for they shall inherit the earth."
> Matthew 5:3-12

These qualities go against everything the world promotes but are the markers of a heart that is surrendered to God's Kingdom.

Our actions should flow from love. Love for God and love for others. Jesus said that the greatest commandment is to love God with all our heart, soul, mind, and strength, and the second is like it: to love our neighbor as ourselves.

> "Jesus replied, 'You must love the Lord your God with all your heart, all your soul, and all your mind.' This is the first and greatest commandment. A second is equally important: 'Love your neighbor as yourself."
> Matthew 22:37-40

This love is not based on how others treat us but on the unconditional love God has shown us. It is a love that extends even to our enemies, as Jesus taught in the Sermon on the Mount.

Living for the Kingdom of God also means we live with an eternal perspective. The world's perspective is short-sighted, focused only on what can be gained here and now, but the Kingdom of God is eternal.

> "And this is eternal life, that they know you, the only true God, and Jesus Christ whom you have sent."
> John 17:3

INTENTIONALLY DESIGNED

Eternal life begins now, the moment we accept Jesus as our Savior and become citizens of Heaven.

Eternity does not start after we die—it is something we enter into the moment we are reborn in Christ. When we understand this, it changes how we live. We stop living for the temporary things of this world and begin living for the things that have eternal significance. We begin to store up treasures in Heaven, not on Earth.

"Don't store up treasures here on earth, where moths eat them and rust destroys them, and where thieves break in and steal. Store your treasures in heaven, where moths and rust cannot destroy, and thieves do not break in and steal. "
Matthew 6:19-21

THE BENEFITS OF KINGDOM LIVING

Living for the Kingdom of God has its benefits. First and foremost, it means we are no longer slaves to fear. As citizens of God's Kingdom, we are empowered by the Holy Spirit, who gives us boldness, love, and self-control (2 Timothy 1:7). Fear no longer has a hold on us because we know God is with us, and His power is made perfect in our weakness.

In God's Kingdom, there's no competition, only cooperation. We are all part of one body, working together for the advancement of the Kingdom.

"For just as the body is one and has many members, and all the members of the body, though many, are one body, so it is with Christ."
1 Corinthians 12:2

We are designed to use our unique gifts for the glory of God and the building up of the Body of Christ. Whether it's serving, teaching, leading, or creating, every gift is essential for the advancement of the Kingdom.

DESIGNED FOR THE KINGDOM OF GOD

LIVING FOR THE KINGDOM HERE AND NOW

The Kingdom of God is not just for church services or conferences. It is for our everyday lives. Whether working, parenting, serving, or just living, we are called to reflect the values of God's Kingdom. We can bring the Kingdom of Heaven to Earth through our actions, words, and relationships.

At work, our integrity, work ethic, and relationships should reflect Kingdom values. At home, we create an environment where love, respect, and godly principles are lived out. In our communities, we can be agents of change, bringing God's justice, mercy, and love to those around us. This is how we bring Heaven to Earth.

But we cannot do this on our own. We need the Holy Spirit to empower us and help us live out our Kingdom calling. It begins with discerning our gifts and calling, developing them through practice and mentorship, and then deploying them to serve others. This is how we bring the Kingdom of God to the world around us.

BACK TO EDEN

When we live for the Kingdom of God, we return to God's original design. The brokenness that entered the world in Eden is being redeemed through Jesus Christ. The Kingdom of God is God's way of restoring what was lost in Eden and inviting us to partner with Him in that restoration.

The world will always try to convince us that living for temporary, earthly things is enough. But as citizens of Heaven, we are called to something far greater: to live for the Kingdom of God, live out His values, and help bring Heaven to Earth. This world is not our home, but the Kingdom of God is. As we live for that Kingdom, we reflect the glory of the One who called us, created us, and sent

INTENTIONALLY DESIGNED

us into this world to bring His light to the darkness.

God has designed you for this Kingdom, and He has equipped you to bring His love, justice, mercy, and humility to the world. Will you embrace your calling as a citizen of Heaven? Will you live with an eternal perspective, knowing that this world is not your home? The Kingdom of God is where you belong. As you align your life with God's purposes, you will experience the fulfillment of being part of something far greater than yourself. Let's live for the Kingdom. Let's bring Heaven to Earth. Amen?

Here's what I know to be true. God made you on purpose, with a purpose for the Kingdom of God to do the good works that God prepared in advance for you to do. God crafted you with such intention to be a vulnerable expression of His love to the world. God didn't create you to show up small but to show up in the fullness that He created you to be. God doesn't send people to places, but people to people. He made you for community, to worship together and cultivate the gardens of life. Many of us feel stuck in the cycle of lies and fear that we have to keep up with the Joneses, that we are not enough, or that we are too much. **You belong in the kingdom of God.**

So, will you live your life for God? Will you go all in? If you're afraid, do it afraid. God is with you. In your weakness, His power is strong and perfected. His grace is sufficient. The body of Christ needs you and the hope you carry. The world needs the kind of light that shines on a hill and shouldn't be hidden. Your Heavenly Father loves you and delights in you. Pray, show up, and be a student of the word of God.

As this book comes to an end, my prayer for you is this: Would you seek God with your whole heart and run after Him and His plan for your life? Would you choose to trust Him in the toughest moments of your life, knowing He's got it, even when we don't understand? Would you see

DESIGNED FOR THE KINGDOM OF GOD

your value as a child of God and help bring Heaven down to Earth? I bless you. I can't wait to see and hear what God does in and through your life. God bless you. May He go before, behind you, beside you, all around you, and within you. He is with you.

-Hannah Castiaux

"It is the LORD who goes before you. He will be with you; he will not leave you or forsake you. Do not fear or be dismayed."
Deuteronomy 31:8

King of Kings,

Thank You for designing me to be part of Your eternal Kingdom. Help me keep my eyes fixed on You and live in a way that reflects my citizenship in heaven. May I pursue things of eternal value, storing up treasures in heaven rather than being distracted by the temporary things of this world. Empower me to live for Your glory, knowing that I am part of something far greater than myself.

In Jesus' name,
Amen.

INTENTIONALLY DESIGNED

RESOURCES

God's Glory In Your Story Podcast
www.godsgloryinyourstory.com/podcast

God's Glory In Your Story Newsletter - Scan QR Code to join!

Spiritual Gifts Assessment: https://gifts.churchgrowth.org/spiritual-gifts-survey/gifts-survey/

Book Resources:
Strength's Finder by Tom Rath
Tired of Being Tired by Jess Connolly
Play Where Your Feet Are by Cameron Dobbs

Citations:
1. Perry, Jackie Hill. *IF Gathering* 2020. IF: Gathering, March 2020. https://www.ifgathering.com.

2. Connolly, J. *Leading & Loving It* 2023. Leading and Loving It Conference, October 2023. https://www.leadingandlovingit.com.

ABOUT THE AUTHOR

Hannah Castiaux is a Christian author, speaker, and host of the God's Glory in Your Story podcast. As a local church leader and passionate advocate for women's ministry, she helps women break free from the lies and labels of the world to live boldly in their God-given purpose. Hannah Castiaux is committed to empowering women to go deeper in their faith and walk in the freedom and identity found in Christ.

INTENTIONALLY DESIGNED